BIG ENGLISH 5 PLUS

Contents

1	MY INTERESTS	4
2	FAMILY TIES	18
3	HELPING OTHERS	32
	Checkpoint Units 1–3	46
4	SHOPPING AROUND	48
5	VACATION TIME	62
6	THE FUTURE	76
	Checkpoint Units 4–6	90
7	WHAT'S THAT?	92
8	WHERE DO THEY COME FROM?	106
9	HOW ADVENTUROUS ARE YOU?	120
	Checkpoint Units 7–9	134
	Extra Grammar Practice	136
	YLE Practice Material	145
	Checkpoint Cutouts	159

Pearson Education Limited
Edinburgh Gate
Harlow
Essex CM20 2JE
England
and Associated Companies throughout the world.

www.pearsonelt.com/bigenglish

© Pearson Education Limited 2015

Authorised adaptation from the United States edition entitled Big English, 1st Edition, by Mario Herrera and Christopher Sol Cruz. Published by Pearson Education Inc. © 2013 by Pearson Education, Inc.

The right of Mario Herrera and Christopher Sol Cruz to be identified as the authors of this Work have been asserted by them in accordance with the Copyright, Designs and Patents Act 1988.

All rights reserved; no part of this publication may be reproduced, stored in a retrieval system, or transmitted in any form or by any means, electronic, mechanical, photocopying, recording, or otherwise without the prior written permission of the Publishers.

First published 2015
Sixth impression 2018

ISBN: 978-1-4479-8954-7

Set in Apex Sans
Editorial production and project management by hyphen S.A.
Printed in China (CTPSC/06)

Acknowledgements
The publisher would like to thank the following for their kind permission to reproduce their photographs:

(Key: b-bottom; c-centre; l-left; r-right; t-top)

Alamy Images: Irene Abdou 28bc, age fotostock 86, Frankie Angel 93/2, Bubbles Photolibrary 67br, Jonah Calinawan 121bc, Mark Conlin 24l, Hilda DeSanctis 97bc, Judy Freilicher 17tl, Tim Gainey 28tc, GOIMAGES 93/1, 105/4, Ruth Hofshi 24br, Image Source 90 (deckchair, sunglasses), Janine Wiedel Photolibrary 12bl, Dennis MacDonald 62br, 70b, Iain Masterton 48bc, mediacolor's 128bc, Mira 4tc, 46t/2, 138t/2, Morgan Lane Photography 32br, 46b/4, 138t/3, Myrleen Pearson 32tl, 40t, 46b/2, 67cr, Lana Rastro 18bl, 27b, 46c/2, 137b, Neil Setchfield 28t, Simon Price 90 (helmet), Sinibomb Images 32tc, 40bl, 46b/1, 138b/1, Steve Vidler 58t; **Brand X Pictures:** Burke Triolo Productions 98t; **Corbis:** Ocean 12br, Jami Tarris 24tr; **DK Images:** Andy Crawford 94tr, Dave King, Andy Crawford 93/4, 100tc, Susanna Price 21; **Fotolia.com:** 2tun 56t, 6ll, 90 (bracelet), Africa Studio 56b, 90 (balloons), alarsonphoto 48tc, 6lr, Aaron Amat 93/3, 100bc, arinahabich 128br, Artur Synenko 111/2, asese 6br, bkhphoto 90 (bottle), BVDC 137t, Jacek Chabraszewski 32bl, Cybrain 111cr, 114c, dja65 97t, 100t, 111tr, DM7 82l, emese73 4tr, 111tl, eurobanks 114l, Gelpi 6l, GoodMood Photo 107tl, 115l, Haslam Photography 48bl, Barbara Helgason 48tr, 90 (frame), Darrin Henry 4bl, 41, 46t/3, Herjua 72t, higyou 82tr, Ken Hurst 45br, 63, 141, JJAVA 120bl, JonMilnes 122t, Kadmy 18tl, 46c/1, kaphotokevm1 18tr, 46c/4, KaYann 106tl, Igor Klimov 42t, 77r, 85bc, 90 (laptop), Mitchell Knapton 67tl, 70c, 92tr, Douglas Knight 111cl, Robert Lerich 120tr, MasterLu 72b, milachka 17tr, 111/3, mirabella 6lc, Monkey Business 4tl, 10r, 62tc, 67bl, 70t, Denis Pepin 107bl, percent 107tr, 115r, petunyia 96tc, 105/2, plutofrosti 77cr, 85t, 90 (tablet), 93 (c), Beatrice Prève 4br, 128bl, prudkov 39r, Denys Prykhodov 77l, Scanrail 102br, 107br, SerrNovik 17bl, skynet 111/1, 143, soundsnaps 105 (a), strelov 94bl, 100b, sumnersgraphicsinc 114r, 119, Milos Tasic 111br, 115c, tuja66 105 (b), Tupungato 112, Simone van den Berg 32tr, 40br, 46b/3, 138b/3, EJ White 45bl, Lisa F. Young 17cl, 138b/2; **Getty Images:** The Image Bank / Terence Langendoen 90 (jacket), Uwe Umstatter 97br; **Glow Images:** Aurora Open / Henry Georgi 62tr, Corbis / Bridge / Jim Cummins 10l, ImageBroker / Ulrich Doering 5, 12tr, 17br, 46t/4, NordicPhotos / Svenne Nordlov 138b/4, PhotoNonStop / Eurasia Press 58b, Uppercut 27t; **Pearson Education Ltd:** Jon Barlow 45tl; **PhotoDisc:** 116b; **PhotoEdit Inc.:** Jeff Greenberg 32bc; **Photoshot Holdings Limited:** C. C. Lockwood 122b; **Reuters:** Borja Suarez 130b; **Rex Features:** David Fisher 30; **Shutterstock.com:** 3Dstock 85b, 90 (phone), 93 (d), 106br, 108, 116t, 126t, alexnika 97tc, Antonio V. Oquias 120br, baitong333 62bc, 67cl, Rudy Balasko 96bc, 105/3, Fernando Blanco Calzada 77cl, 85tc, 90 (MP3 player), 93 (b), bonchan 12lt, Boonsom 106tr, Patrick Breig 50, 82br, Carlos Caetano 16, 96b, Jacek Chabraszewski 57, Norman Chan 120tl, Oleksandr Chub 105 (c), Melanie DeFazio 18bc, Ersler Dmitry 93 (a), Michelle Eadie 130t, eurobanks 6tr, 45tr, 89, fet 4bc, 12tl, 46t/1, Natali Glado 48br, higyou 102tr, HomeStudio 97b (abacus), Imagebroker.net 54, Robert Kneschke 18tc, 46c/3, Susan Leggett 62tr, 67tr, 70tc, marekuliasz 48tl, 60, 90 (headphones), marylooo 138t/1, MaszaS 62bl, MaxyM 128t, naluwan 39l, Nata-Lia 96t, 105/1, Natursports 126b, Ociacia 92tl, Daniel Padavona 121b, PRILL 92bl, rprongjai 121tc, Renata Sedmakova 101l, 106bl, Elzbieta Sekowska 129, Charles Taylor 78, Michael J Thompson 101r, Tomasz Trojanowski 17cr, 51, Wallenrock 28b, Ivonne Wierink 42b, Michael Woodruff 14, Mikhail Zahranichny 70bc, Peter Zvonar 99; **Sozaijiten:** 102bl; **SuperStock:** Exactostock 71, imagebroker.net 92br; **Werner Forman Archive Ltd:** 95

Cover images: Front: **Shutterstock.com:** Charlie Hutton l, Elzbieta Sekowska c; **SuperStock:** Fancy Collection r

All other images © Pearson Education

Every effort has been made to trace the copyright holders and we apologise in advance for any unintentional omissions. We would be pleased to insert the appropriate acknowledgement in any subsequent edition of this publication.

Illustrated by
Zaharias Papadopoulos (hyphen), Q2A Media Services, Anthony Lewis, Christos Skaltsas (hyphen).

Big English Song

From the mountaintops to the bottom of the sea,
From a big blue whale to a baby bumblebee –
If you're big, if you're small, you can have it all,
And you can be anything you want to be!

It's bigger than you. It's bigger than me.
There's so much to do, and there's so much to see!
The world is big and beautiful, and so are we!
Think big! Dream big! Big English!

So in every land, from the desert to the sea
We can all join hands and be one big family.
If we love, if we care, we can go anywhere!
The world belongs to everyone; it's ours to share.

It's bigger than you. It's bigger than me.
There's so much to do, and there's so much to see!
The world is big and beautiful, and so are we!
Think big! Dream big! Big English!

It's bigger than you. It's bigger than me.
There's so much to do, and there's so much to see!
The world is big and beautiful and waiting for me.
A one, two, three...
Think big! Dream big! Big English!

unit 1
MY INTERESTS

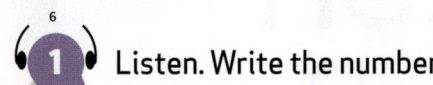

1 Listen. Write the number.

☐ a reading ☐ b painting

☐ c playing chess ☐ d playing the guitar

☐ e doing martial arts ☐ f playing soccer

2 Look at the pictures in 1. Which of the activities do people usually do alone (A)? Which do they usually do with others (O)? Which do they sometimes do both alone and with others (AO)? Write A, O, or AO.

1 ____   2 ____   3 ____
4 ____   5 ____   6 ____

3 Which of the activities in 1 do you do in your free time? Write the numbers.

_____

4 Unit 1

4 Match the interests to the school groups. Write the letter.

Interests
_____ 1 martial arts
_____ 2 acting
_____ 3 writing articles
_____ 4 playing music
_____ 5 building things

School Groups
a drama club
b science club
c school orchestra
d school newspaper
e tae kwon do club

5 What are you good at? What school group do you want to join? Complete the sentences.

I'm good at _____.
I want to join _____.

What school group could they join?

Susan can move really fast. _____

James is good at taking pictures. _____

Elizabeth won a prize for a play she wrote. _____

David's really interested in technology. _____

Anna plays the violin really well. _____

Richard's the best singer in our class. _____

Reading | Online newsletter

 **6** Listen and read. Then answer the questions.

Manbury School News Opinion Page

Home | For Teachers | For Students | School Directory | Clubs

DO WHAT'S RIGHT FOR YOU

bbrown

It's a new school year. Everyone is talking about the new after-school clubs because they're fun. You can learn new things and make new friends. But some students aren't interested in joining clubs. They may be shy or scared of groups. These students might be good at singing or playing an instrument but they like doing these activities alone. They don't want to join clubs, and that's fine.

I'm a shy girl. I enjoy watching sports on TV, painting, and playing my guitar. I'm not interested in joining a sports team, art club, or the school orchestra. My friends were upset with me because I didn't want to join their clubs, so I talked to my mom about it. She said, "It's OK. Be yourself. Do the things you like to do." I want to say to shy children like me, "Do what's right for you. Find friends who are like you. You don't always have to do what everyone else does."

Comments

Silver

I'm shy, too. I always feel bad when my classmates talk about signing up for after-school clubs. I'm glad to know that I'm not the only one.

suki.park

Wow! I love clubs, and I never thought some children might not want to join them. Thanks for writing this. Personally, I don't like doing things alone, so clubs are good for me.

1. What's this newsletter about?

2. Is the newsletter writer interested in joining clubs? Why/Why not?

3. What does she enjoy doing?

4. Is bbrown shy?

7 What do you think about the newsletter? Write your own comment.

6 Unit 1

Language in Action

8 Listen. Then read and circle **T** for true and **F** for false.

Cathy: Are you interested in joining a club this year, Ben?

Ben: <u>I don't know</u>… I don't have much time. I usually have homework. And when I have free time, I read my manga comic books.

Cathy: Manga? Those Japanese comic books? Cool! Hey, did you hear that there's a manga club at school this year?

Ben: <u>Really?</u>

Cathy: Yes, really! You can sign up in Mr. West's room.

Ben: Where did you hear about it? When does it meet?

Cathy: Ken told me about it. I joined yesterday! It meets on Wednesdays and Fridays.

Ben: Oh, good. I can do that. <u>Count me in!</u>

Cathy: <u>Great!</u> See you there tomorrow.

1 Ben has a lot of free time.   T   F
2 The manga club meets twice a week.   T   F
3 Ben's going to join the manga club.   T   F
4 Cathy hasn't joined the manga club.   T   F

9 Look at **8**. Read the underlined expressions. How can you say them in other words? Match and write the letter.

____ 1 I don't know.   **a** This is good news.
____ 2 Really?   **b** I'll be there!
____ 3 Count me in!   **c** I can't believe it's true!
____ 4 Great!   **d** I'm not sure what I want to do.

10 Complete the sentences with the expressions in **9**. Then listen and check your answers.

A: Our class is going to Rome for our class trip.

B: ¹_____! How exciting! When do you leave?

A: Tomorrow morning at 4 a.m.

B: ²_____? That's crazy! How will you wake up that early?

A: ³_____. I hope Mom will wake me up! Hey, why don't you come to the airport with us?

B: Why not? It'll be fun! ⁴_____!

Unit 1   7

Language in Action

> How about **joining** the drama club? No, thanks. I'm not good at **acting**.
> How about **trying out** for the basketball team? OK. I love **playing** basketball.

11 Look at the pictures of Sue and Kevin. Complete the sentences. Use the correct form of the verbs from the box.

> do tae kwon do   play chess   play soccer   take pictures

1 Sue and Kevin both enjoy _____.
2 Sue enjoys _____. Kevin isn't interested in it.
3 Sue has a good camera. She likes _____.
4 Kevin enjoys martial arts. He loves _____.

12 Complete the sentences. Circle the correct form of the verbs.

1 **A:** How about **tries / trying** out for the basketball team?
  B: I'm not sure. I'm not very good at **playing / play** basketball.
2 **A:** How about **joining / you join** the tae kwon do club?
  B: Great! I love **do / doing** martial arts.
3 **A:** How about **join / joining** the drama club?
  B: I don't know. I'm not very interested in **acts / acting**.
4 **A:** How about **goes / going** to the new action movie with me on Saturday?
  B: Well, maybe. But I don't really like **watching / watches** action movies.

Language in Action

13 Write the questions. Use **How about** and the words from the box.

audition for/school play   join/school news bloggers   join/science club   try out for/track team

1 **Paul:** _____
   Nora: Good idea! I really enjoy playing sports.

2 **Paul:** _____
   Nora: I don't know. I'm not very good at acting.

3 **Paul:** _____
   Nora: That's a good idea. I'm good at math, and I love doing projects.

4 **Paul:** _____
   Nora: Sounds great! I enjoy writing!

14 Complete the sentences about a friend. Use **he** or **she**.

My friend's name is _____. _____ likes _____, and _____'s good at _____. _____ isn't interested in _____, but _____ and I enjoy _____.

15 Read the questions. Write answers for yourself.

1 How about trying out for the soccer team?
   _____

2 How about signing up for the book club?
   _____

3 How about joining the science club?
   _____

Unit 1   9

Content Connection | Science

16 Match the words to the definitions. Write the letters.

1. personality
2. brain
3. control
4. analyze
5. solve
6. creative
7. hemisphere
8. logical

a good at thinking of new ideas
b the unique combination of traits that characterize a person
c the part of your body that controls how you think, feel, and move
d find the answer to a problem
e one of two halves of a sphere or brain
f make someone or something do what you want
g reasonable and sensible
h examine something carefully in order to understand it

17 Listen and read. Who likes making lists?

Left Brained or Right Brained?

Tom

"I have a left-brained personality. This means that the left hemisphere of my brain is stronger than the right hemisphere. Some scientists believe that this stronger side of my brain may help, in some ways, determine what I'm good at, what I'm interested in, and what I like to do. For example, I'm really good at solving math problems. I like to analyze things and to think logically. I like working alone, too. I enjoy writing, but I'm not good at being creative. I'm very organized, so I like listening and taking notes in class. I usually remember the details when I read. As I study, I write things down and make lists. It helps me remember."

Sara

"Honestly, I'm the opposite of Tom. I'm definitely more right brained than left brained! This means that the right hemisphere of my brain is stronger than my left hemisphere. So, for example, I'm imaginative and creative. I like making up and telling stories. I love drawing, dancing, and playing music. I enjoy working in groups and solving problems together. I like surprises, but I'm not good at organizing things. Sometimes I talk when I shouldn't in class, and I get distracted when I should be listening. When I study, I draw pictures because it helps me remember. I'm not very good at remembering details or making lists, though."

18 Read 17 again and circle Tom or Sara.

1. Who likes doing projects in groups? — **Tom** **Sara**
2. Who should be a member of the drama club? — **Tom** **Sara**
3. Who should be a school news blogger? — **Tom** **Sara**
4. Who's probably quieter in class? — **Tom** **Sara**
5. Who's probably better at chess? — **Tom** **Sara**
6. Who would enjoy painting a class mural? — **Tom** **Sara**

19 Complete the sentences. Use some of the words in 16.

1. The _____ has two sides – left and right.
2. Each side of our brain is called a _____.
3. Each side of our brain controls different parts of our _____.
4. Can you _____ math problems easily? You might be left brained.
5. Do you enjoy being _____? Then you might be right brained.
6. Left-brained people are better at _____ thinking than right-brained people.

THINK BIG

What kinds of jobs are left-brained people and right-brained people more suited to? Write the jobs in the chart. Add another job to each column.

computer programmer   drama teacher   fashion designer
make-up artist   scientist   vet

Left-brained	Right-brained

Unit 1   11

Culture Connection | Around the World

26 Complete the sentences with words from the box.

> compete   competitor   dangerous   fearless   racing   sporting event

1 Bike races can be _____ because the riders go very fast.
2 Swimming is a _____ at the Olympics.
3 My favorite _____ is the young man from Kenya.
4 You have to be _____ when skiing down those high mountains!
5 My father enjoys watching bike _____ more than any other sport on TV.
6 If you want to _____ in this sport, you have to be a very good swimmer.

27 Listen and read. Match the headings A–C to the paragraphs 1–3.

A Bunny Hops and Whoops   B Dangerous Olympic Sports   C Competing in a BMX Race

New Olympic Sport

1
Some Olympic sports are more dangerous than others. For example, sports that are very fast are often more dangerous than those that are slower. Do you like riding your bike fast? Did you know that extra fast bike riding is a sport in the Olympics? Bike racing started as an Olympic sport in Athens in 1896. Over the years, there were road races and track races and mountain-bike racing in the Olympic Games. Then, in the 2008 Beijing Games, a bike sport called BMX became a new Olympic sport. BMX started in California in about 1968. The sport grew, and now it is a favorite sport for many people around the world. It's a very fast and dangerous sport, so competitors have to be fearless to take part!

2
Both men and women compete in BMX. The bikes they use are light and very strong. They need to be strong enough for all the jumps and ramps, and yet remain light, so the riders can travel as fast as possible. The tracks for men are about 450 meters long. They're a little shorter for women. But this doesn't mean that the women's races take less time than the men's races. All the races last only forty seconds! If you blink, you'll miss them!

3
Like any sport, BMX racing has its own special words. The riders have created new words to talk about their sport, such as "bunny hop." A bunny hop is when a rider's bike goes up in the air. The rider in the picture is bunny hopping. You can see how high he goes and how important it is for his bike to be both light and strong. Another special word is "whoop." A whoop is a small bump in the road. So, the next time you ride your bike, watch out for whoops and don't bunny hop. Stay safe!

14 Unit 1

28 Read 27 again and rewrite the sentences so that they are true.

1 Only men compete in BMX.
   _____

2 The bikes are heavy.
   _____

3 Each race lasts sixty seconds.
   _____

4 A bunny hop is a small bump in the road.
   _____

29 Find these numbers in 27. Write the sentences with these numbers.

1 eighteen ninety-six
   _____

2 nineteen sixty-eight
   _____

3 four hundred and fifty
   _____

30 Unscramble and write the words from 26.

1 _____ pmcoiterot
2 _____ slsrafee
3 _____ gnicra
4 _____ regnaduso
5 _____ sintgpor netve
6 _____ teepomc

THINK BIG Why is BMX dangerous? Do all people enjoy doing dangerous sports? Why/Why not?

_____

Unit 1 15

Writing | News article

A good news article includes important information about an event. It includes the answers to these questions: *Who* is the article about? *What* is the article about? *When* did the event happen? *Where* did the event happen? *What happened*?

A good news article also gives other information to make the story interesting, but don't forget to answer the questions!

KEY QUESTIONS:
Who?
What?
When?
Where?
What happened?

31 Read the answers (A). Complete the questions (Q) with Who, What, When, Where, or What happened.

1. Q: _____? You're all dirty!
   A: I slipped and fell in the mud!

2. Q: _____ does the club meet?
   A: It meets in the science lab.

3. Q: _____'s that over there?
   A: That's my science club leader.

4. Q: _____ does the science club meet?
   A: It meets on Mondays after school.

5. Q: _____ do you do in science club?
   A: We play chess and other fun games.

32 Write a news article. Use the information in the chart. Add interesting information.

Who?	What?	When?	Where?	What happened?
People who enjoy acting	Audition for the musical *Peter Pan*	Last Monday after school	In the auditorium	More than 20 students auditioned

Interesting Information:
Everyone was nervous. Mr. Bannister's going to post the results on the school website.

THINK BIG

Write Who? What? When? Where? What happened?

Add some interesting information.

_____ It rained.
_____ Played in a concert.
_____ Hampton School orchestra.
_____ At Green Park.
_____ On Saturday morning.

16 Unit 1

Review

33 Where do these activities <u>usually</u> take place? Write the words in the correct column.

> act on stage   do track   play in an orchestra
> play soccer   play the piano   write articles

Inside	Outside
_____	_____
_____	_____
_____	_____

34 Write questions with **how about** and the words in parentheses. Then look at the pictures and complete the answers.

1 **Peggy:** Carla, _____
 _____?
 (try out for/basketball team)
 Carla: I don't think so! You know I only play
 _____.

2 **James:** Olivia, _____
 _____?
 (sign up for/school newspaper)
 Olivia: Great idea! I really enjoy
 _____.

3 **Marco:** _____
 _____?
 (join/the school orchestra)
 Daniel: No, I can't play an instrument, but I'm interested in _____.
 Maybe I'll join the drama club.

Unit 1 17

unit 2
FAMILY TIES

1 Match the pictures to the sentences. Write the number.

☐ The couple got married.   ☐ The student graduated from college.

☐ The family moved to a new house.   ☐ The family opened a restaurant.

☐ The baby was born at 5 a.m.

2 Answer the questions about your family. Circle Yes or No.

Last year:

1	Did your family open a store or restaurant?	Yes	No
2	Did you move to a new home?	Yes	No
3	Did a family member graduate from university or college?	Yes	No
4	Was a new family member born?	Yes	No
5	Did a family member get married?	Yes	No

3 Match and complete the phrases. Write the words.

1 graduated   a _____ to a new place
2 moved   b _____ from business school
3 got   c _____ born
4 opened   d _____ a store
5 was   e _____ married

4  Listen to the events in Ken's life. Then number the timeline in order and write the events.

TIMELINE OF KEN'S LIFE	
	Age 25 _____
	Age 44 _____
	Age 21 _____
	Age 0 _____
	Age 28 _____

THINK BIG

Write the words for these family members. Use aunt, brother, sister, or uncle.

My mom's sister is my _____.
My dad's brother is my _____.
My aunt is my dad's _____.
My uncle is my mom's _____.

Unit 2 19

Reading | Autobiographical Story

5 Listen and read. Then answer the questions.

My Amazing Family

My name is Theresa, and I have an unusual and amazing family. We're superheroes! We can do amazing things, and we like to help people.

My mom was born in Venice, and she moved to Barcelona in 1996. My dad was born in Barcelona. He met my mom there when they both helped save people in a house fire. They got married in 2000 and had three children soon after that. I'm the oldest child, and I have a younger brother, Tomas, and a baby sister, Tara. Tomas is eight. I'm stronger than him. I can pick up a car! But Tomas is faster than me. He can run a kilometer in less than 15 seconds! That's really fast! Tara is incredible! She can make herself very, very small, sometimes smaller than a peanut. That's why we call her "Peanut." I love my family because we're always doing exciting things.

1 Why is this family amazing?
_____

2 Where was Theresa's mom born?
_____

3 Where did Theresa's parents meet?
_____

4 Who's the oldest child in the family?
_____

5 Why does the family call Tara "Peanut"?
_____

6 Answer the questions.

1 What special power would you like to have? Why?
_____

2 What are you going to do with your special power?
_____

Language in Action

7 Listen. Then circle the correct answers.

Will: Oh… this is a great picture! What a cute baby!
Deb: Guess who… ?
Will: No! That's not you! Is it?
Deb: Yes… that's me. That's the day I was born.
Will: That's nice. But… what happened?
Deb: What do you mean?
Will: You were so much cuter then!
Deb: Ha, ha! Very funny. My mother says I was the cutest baby in the world.
Will: Well, I don't know…. But you were pretty cute.
Deb: Thanks.

1 Who's the baby in the picture?
   a someone in Will's family   b Deb

2 Will _____ when he says that Deb was cuter when she was a baby.
   a is serious   b is joking

3 Deb's mom said that she was the cutest baby in the world. Will _____.
   a agrees   b doesn't really agree

8 Look at 7. Read the underlined expressions. How can you say them in other words? Match and write the letters.

_____ 1 That's nice.
_____ 2 What do you mean?
_____ 3 Ha, ha! Very funny.
_____ 4 Well, I don't know…

a I don't understand what you're talking about.
b That's not funny.
c I don't think that's exactly true.
d I like it.

9 Circle the correct expressions.

1 **A:** That's a picture of my brother.
   B: That's nice. / Well, I don't know. You look exactly like him!
   A: Yes, we do because we're twins!

2 **A:** That's the day we moved.
   B: What do you mean? / Ha, ha! Very funny.
   A: We moved from Norwich to Oxford.
   B: I didn't know that!

Unit 2 21

Language in Action

> We **went** to Edinburgh <u>when</u> I **was** eight.
> <u>When</u> they **were** children, they **lived** in Manchester.
> She **moved** to Cambridge three years <u>ago</u>.
> A few months <u>later</u>, she **got** a new job.

10 Find and circle each past tense verb. There are ten verbs.

wasfhadgwgotnwereuytwentmlivedopmovedtfoundkjfboughtwstartedqcworkedm

11 Look at **10**. Write the past tense form of the verbs.

be	_____	have	_____
buy	_____	live	_____
find	_____	move	_____
get	_____	start	_____
go	_____	work	_____

12 Complete the paragraph. Use the correct form of the verbs in **11**.

My mom and dad ¹_____ married when they ²_____ 24. They ³_____ with my dad's parents because they ⁴_____ to save money to buy their own house. They both ⁵_____ long hours at their jobs. A few years later, they ⁶_____ a house. That ⁷_____ 15 years ago. They ⁸_____ into the house on my mom's birthday. I ⁹_____ born a year later!

22 Unit 2

Language in Action

> Sue's **taller than** Yoko and Mark.
> Sue's **the tallest** person in our class.

 13 Listen and number the family members.

14 Look at the picture. Complete the sentences. Use the correct form of the words in parentheses.

1. (tall) Joan's _____.
   Ben's _____ than Joan.
   Ben's _____ child.

2. (young) Maria's _____.
   Maria's _____ Joan and Ben. Maria's _____ child.

3. (long) Maria's hair is _____ Ben's hair. Joan's hair is _____ hair of all.

15 Think of a good friend. How are you different? Write sentences. Use the words from the box.

> big   new   old   strong   tall

1 _____
2 _____
3 _____

Unit 2 23

Content Connection | Science

16 Read the definitions. Circle the correct word.

1 An animal's child or children	**offspring**	predator
2 To prevent something from being harmed	hunt	**protect**
3 An animal that kills and eats other animals	**predator**	young
4 Animals that are not old	**young**	pouch
5 To catch and kill animals	**hunt**	protect
6 The part of an animal's body where it carries its babies	**pouch**	offspring

17 Read and complete. Then listen and check.

> eggs   food   mother   predators   protect   young

Good and Bad Dads in the Animal Kingdom

Just like your mom, your dad is a special and important person in your family. Think of all the things that your dad does for you. Many dads work hard to pay for the things that their families need. They also do many things at home to help take care of their children.

Fathers are important in the animal kingdom, too. They take care of their families and some even take care of other families. But some fathers are better than others.

1. The father emu is a great dad. He finds grass, twigs, and leaves. Then he builds a nest for his **1**_____ all by himself. He sits on the eggs until the baby chicks are born. During this time, he doesn't eat or drink! When the chicks are born, the dad takes care of them and teaches them how to find **2**_____.

2. The father seahorse gives birth to his young! He does something very special to **3**_____ his future offspring. He carries the **4**_____ in a special pouch on the front of his tail for about three weeks until the baby seahorses are born. What an amazing dad!

3. Lions are fierce **5**_____ and can be really scary! A father lion protects his family, and his family can be big. There can be seven lionesses (**6**_____ lions) and twenty babies in his family. But he isn't really a great dad. He doesn't often hunt for food. The moms have to do that. The father lion likes to sleep a lot, especially on branches in trees. He's lazy!

18 Read **17** again and answer the questions.

1 What does the father emu use to build his nest?
_____

2 When does the father emu not eat or drink?
_____

3 What amazing thing does the father seahorse do?
_____

4 How does the father seahorse carry the eggs?
_____

5 What does the father lion do for his family?
_____

6 Why is the lion not a very good dad?
_____

19 Complete the sentences with words from the box.

> hunt   offspring   pouch   predators   protecting

1 Many animal fathers help to take care of their _____.
2 Some animal parents take turns _____ their eggs.
3 Lionesses teach their young how to _____ for their food.
4 Some kinds of animals in Australia have a _____ on the front of their body.
5 Lions, leopards, and cheetahs are _____ because they kill and eat smaller animals.

THINK BIG

What things do human fathers do to take care of their children? Make a list.

- _____   - _____
- _____   - _____
- _____   - _____

Unit 2 **25**

Grammar

20 Read and circle.

1 I **used to / didn't use to** love reading books about animals, but now I love adventure books.
2 She **used to / didn't use to** live in France because she's always lived next door.
3 They **used to / didn't use to** visit their grandparents on Sundays, but now they've moved.
4 You **used to / didn't use to** catch the bus much, but now I often see you at the bus stop.
5 We **used to / didn't use to** go to the beach in the summer, but now we go hiking every year.

21 Read and match.

1 Did you use to live in New York?
2 Did he use to play basketball?
3 Did they use to live on a farm?
4 Did we use to eat our snacks inside?
5 Did I use to speak loudly?

a Yes, they did. It was very big.
b No, we didn't. We ate outside.
c Yes, you did. You were very noisy!
d Yes, I did. I loved that city!
e No, he didn't. He used to play tennis.

22 Complete Cara's email to her cousin. Use **used to** or **didn't use to** with a verb from the box.

go   have   send   wait   watch   write

To: Tanya.B@buzzmail.com
From: Cara_Tomms@telefunk.com
Subject: Guess what Grandma said!

Hi Tanya,

Hope things are okay. I called Grandma yesterday, and we started to talk about her past. She told me all these amazing things. Guess what! When Grandma was young, she ¹_____ letters by hand and mail them. Then she ²_____ for a few days or even a few weeks to get an answer! People ³_____ emails then. People didn't have computers or cell phones, either. In fact, they ⁴_____ telephones at all in their homes. Can you imagine? They ⁵_____ to the post office or store and pay money to make a phone call. And, guess what! Grandma didn't use to have a TV or DVD player at home. She ⁶_____ movies at the movie theater in her town. I never knew these things about Grandma's past. Did you?

Love,
Cara

23 Look at the information about Leyla's family. Write one sentence about each person with *used to*.

	Five years ago
Leyla	went to Sweet Valley Elementary School
Leyla's dad	worked as a chef in a restaurant
Leyla's mom	worked in the college library
Leyla's brother	played the trumpet

1 Leyla _____
2 Leyla's dad _____
3 Leyla's mom _____
4 Leyla's brother _____

24 Rewrite the sentences in **23** in the negative. Use *didn't use to*.

1 _____
2 _____
3 _____
4 _____

25 Write four questions to ask your grandparents about the past. Use *Did you use to…?*.

1	
2	
3	
4	

Culture Connection | Around the World

26 Read and match.

1. celebrate
2. decorate
3. tradition
4. symbolize
5. treat

a. something special that you give someone
b. an activity that has been done in a particular way for many years
c. to do something enjoyable on a special occasion
d. to make something attractive by adding things to it
e. to represent an idea or quality

27 Listen and read. Match paragraphs 1-4 to pictures a-d. Who eats Fairy Bread on their birthday?

Special Birthdays

Do you celebrate your birthday? Is there a special tradition in your family or in your culture for birthdays? Many cultures around the world celebrate birthdays – in many different ways. Some cultures celebrate by giving treats to the birthday boy or girl. Other cultures celebrate by doing something special that symbolizes the child's special day. Read on to find out more about how some children around the world celebrate their birthday.

1. In Nigeria, first, fifth, tenth, and fifteenth birthdays are very important. Many parents have big parties for their children and more than 1,000 people come. They eat a lot – sometimes a whole roasted cow!

2. A lot of Brazilian children have fun birthdays. Some parents decorate the house with brightly colored banners and flowers. Brazilians also pull on the ear of the birthday boy or girl. They pull once for each year.

3. On the first birthday of all Hindu children in India, the parents shave the top of their child's head. When they are older, they have birthday parties. They wear new clothes and give thanks to their parents by touching their parents' feet. At school, the birthday child gives chocolate to classmates.

4. Australian children have very sweet birthdays! They eat Fairy Bread. This is a slice of bread and butter covered with small sugary sprinkles called hundreds and thousands.

28 Read **27** again and circle **T** for true and **F** for false.

1. Fifth, tenth, fifteenth, and twentieth birthdays are important in Nigeria.   T   F
2. Sometimes people in Nigeria roast a cow for a special birthday.   T   F
3. Brazilian parents sometimes decorate the house on their child's birthday.   T   F
4. Brazilians pull twice on a child's ear for each year of his or her birthday.   T   F
5. When Hindu children in India turn one, their parents shave the top of their heads.   T   F
6. Australian children have fairy cakes on their birthdays.   T   F

29 Find and circle the words in **26**.

```
              q z i w
          a x c b w j t k
        s y m b o l i z e d
        u d p z p a r a w e
      a t r a d i t i o n c m
      i u m p m r s p t c o n
      l s f u b l w g r p r b
      q u p l x y e f e j a v
      a a e a g l e d a t t c
        c e l e b r a t e e s
        t a s t y a a s y
              i m v l j l
```

How do people celebrate birthdays in your culture?
Which birthdays are important?

_____
_____
_____

Writing | Autobiography

An autobiography describes the important events in your life and when they happened. The events are in the order they happened. The information often includes:
- when and where you were born
- places you lived
- things you did
- your family and friends
- special memories
- your interests

30 Look at Adele's autobiography. Add events from the chart. Use the correct form of the verbs.

Dates	Events
1988	be born in London, England
1991	start singing
2006	write my first successful songs
2009	win the Grammy Award for Best New Artist
2011	have throat surgery
2009 to the present	start donating to charities

My Life

My name is Adele. My full name is Adele Laurie Blue Adkins. ¹ _____ _____ in 1988. I'm an only child. I don't have any brothers or sisters, so my mom and I are very close. I ² _____ in front of my mom's friends when I was only three. I loved music and ³ _____ when I was at the BRIT School for Performing Arts and Technology. I was about 18 years old. Three years later, ⁴ _____. That was in 2009.
I ⁵ _____, but I'm fine now and continue to sing and receive awards for my work. In 2009, I ⁶ _____ that help sick children and families of sick children and to charities that help musicians in need.

31 In the Student's Book, you were asked to write a story about your life. Now write a different, imaginary story about your life. Complete the chart below and use it to help you write.

Date	Event
_____	_____
_____	_____
_____	_____
_____	_____

Review

32 Complete the sentences. Use the correct form of the verbs from the box.

> be born   buy   get married   move   start

Notes about my family

1. My brother used to have a very old car, but he _____ a new car last month. He's very happy.
2. I miss my grandma and grandad. They used to live with us, but a year ago, they _____ away, and now they live in Cornwall.
3. My cousin _____ art school last year. He's a really good artist.
4. I have a new baby brother. He _____ a few weeks ago. He looks like me!
5. When my parents _____, they were very young. They used to walk to college together!

33 Complete the sentences. Use **when** or **later** and the correct form of the verbs.

When?	Age 16	Age 17	Age 18	Age 19	Age 21
What happened?	learn to drive	get a part-time job	start college	buy first car	graduate

1. Jack _____ to drive _____ he _____ 16.
2. He _____ a part-time job _____ he _____ 17.
3. _____ he _____ 18, he _____ college.
4. One year _____, he _____ his first car. He _____ 19.
5. He _____ two years _____, and now he works at a bank.

34 Complete the dialog. Use the correct form of the words in parentheses.

A: Tell me about your family, David.

B: Well, I have three sisters, Jen, Beth, and Kim. Jen is [1] _____ of the three. (old) Beth is [2] _____. (young) And Kim is in the middle.

A: That's nice.

B: Yes. And guess what? Beth is [3] _____ in my family! (tall)

Unit 2   31

unit 3
HELPING OTHERS

1 Which activities do you see in the pictures? Write the numbers.

☐ have a cake sale
☐ organize an outdoor activities day
☐ clean up a place
☐ build homes
☐ donate clothes
☐ walk to raise money
☐ tutor or teach someone
☐ make things for a fundraising activity
☐ wash cars

2 Look at 1. Which fundraising activity would these people be best at doing? Write the numbers.

1 Maria likes cleaning up. She's good at organizing things. ☐
2 Carlos loves math. He's really good at explaining things. ☐
3 Jason likes being outdoors. He loves running, swimming, and bike riding. ☐
4 Emma loves baking cookies and cupcakes. She enjoys baking for other people. ☐

32 Unit 3

3 Unscramble and write the words.

1
rta ifar
_____

2
ekca lesa
_____

3
ehva a tccnoer
_____

4
eakm a diove
_____

5
meak soteprs
_____

6
erwti na riatlce
_____

4 Complete the sentences with the words in **3**. Then listen and check your answers.

1 Why don't we have a _____ next week at school? I can make cookies, and you could make a cake.
2 Sara knows how to use the video camera. She can _____ to tell people about our event.
3 We could _____ to make money. A lot of us love to play music.
4 We could _____ and hang them up around school.
5 Let's draw and paint some things and sell them at an _____.
6 Someone could _____ for the school website.

Grade 6 at your school wants to raise money for a local children's hospital. What could they do? How could they tell people about it?

_____

_____

Reading | School blog

5 Listen and read. Then answer the questions.

On Monday, September 25th at 2:30 p.m., Alex in Grade 6 wrote...

WE NEED MONEY!

Listen, everyone. As you know, our school needs a lot of things. We need new computers for the computer lab, a new freezer for the kitchen, and new chess sets for the chess club. There will soon be some fundraising activities to raise money. Fundraising events are often boring, I know. But I think we could be more creative and do some fun things. I talked to some students, and here are some of the best ideas:

- Karaoke competition with children and parents. We can sell tickets to each contestant, and parents and children can compete against each other.
- Temporary tattoos. We could sell tattoos of cartoon characters and other fun things.
- Students vs. teachers sports events. I'd love to see this! We could play basketball or ping-pong... . Any other suggestions for sports?
- Parents' spelling quiz. Let's have our parents spell words! Could your parent win?

What do you think? Let me know. We can talk to our teachers and see if they like the ideas. Maybe we could come up with a fundraising plan for this year that's really fun!

COMMENTS

arichards
Great ideas! I'll help you! Talk to you later.

carrie_thomas
The karaoke night is a fantastic idea! I know my parents would be interested.

1 What's the blog about?

2 What does the writer think about past fundraising activities?

3 What does the writer think about the fundraising plan for this year?

6 What new fundraising ideas do you have? Add a comment.

34 Unit 3

Language in Action

7 Listen. Then circle the correct answers.

Pete: That car looks great! What's going on?

Mary: Oh, thanks. We're doing this car wash to raise money for our science club. We're going to buy materials for our science projects.

Pete: It's a shame you don't have many people or cars.

Mary: Yes. I guess a lot of people don't realize we're doing this here.

Pete: I have an idea. Tim and I could make signs and hold them up over there so that more people will stop.

Mary: What a great idea! We didn't think of that!

1 What's the science club going to do with the money?
   a buy materials for science projects
   b give the money to charity
2 How many people and cars are there?
   a a lot
   b not a lot
3 Does Mary like Pete's idea?
   a yes
   b no
4 What are Tim and Pete going to do?
   a help wash cars
   b make signs and hold them up

8 Find the expressions in 7. Then circle the best meaning of each expression.

1 What's going on?
   a How are you?
   b What are you doing?
2 It's a shame.
   a It's unfortunate.
   b It's fortunate.
3 What a great idea!
   a I like your idea a lot.
   b I'm not sure what your idea is.

9 Complete the dialogs with the expressions in 8.

1 **A:** Hey, Lisa. _____?
   B: I'm cleaning up. What are you doing?
2 **A:** I know what we could do to make money. We could sell raffle tickets.
   B: _____. I like it a lot!
3 **A:** _____ you aren't going to be at the concert tomorrow night.
   B: I know. But I'm really sick. Have a good time without me!

Language in Action

| How **could** we raise money for our club? | We **could** have a car wash. |
| How much **could** they charge to wash one car? | They **could** charge $10 for a small car. For a bigger car, they **could** charge $15. |

10 Complete the questions. Use How could or How much could. Then match the questions to the suggestions. Write the numbers.

1 Let's raise money for a class trip. _____ we raise in two months?

    ____ a We could write articles about it in the school newspaper.

2 _____ we charge for our winter concert tickets?

    ____ b We could have a car wash.

3 _____ we tell people about the art fair?

    ____ c I think we could raise a lot of money.

4 _____ we raise money to buy new soccer shirts?

    ____ d We could probably ask for $10 a ticket.

11 Read the sentences. Complete the sign-up sheet. Write the correct name. Then complete the sentences with could.

The Art Club Book Sale Sign-Up Sheet

Team 1: Collect books on Monday after school	Team 2: Make posters on Tuesday after school	Team 3: Put up posters on Wednesday morning	Team 4: Sell books on Saturday	Team 5: Clean up on Saturday at 4:00
1 Jill	1 Gina	1 Carolyn	9:00–11:00: Tanya	1 Sophie
2 Samantha	2 Ben	2 _____	11:00–1:00 _____	2 Josh
3 _____	3 _____		1:00–3:00: Claire	3 _____

1 Anna is free on Saturday at 11:00. She _____.

2 Paul is free after school on Monday. He _____.

3 Sally is free on Tuesday after school. She _____.

4 Mario is free on Saturday at 4:00. He _____.

5 Lisa is free on Wednesday morning. She _____.

12 Look at 11. Think about your school week. How and when could you help?

_____

Language in Action

> How **are you going to** tell people about your cake sale?
> We**'re going to** make posters.

13 Complete the sentences. Use **am**/**is**/**are going to**.

Grade 6 News

Hi Everyone!

This is a busy week! Our class car wash is this Saturday! We ¹_____ meet in front of the school at 7:30 a.m. Please be on time. Bring a towel and an extra set of clothes – you ²_____ get very wet. I ³_____ bring snacks.

Also, Carol ⁴_____ make posters this Thursday. I hope you can help her. And Jeremy ⁵_____ hand out flyers to parents.

Now we need YOU. Join us! How ⁶_____ we _____ make this a success without you? Can you help? Let me know. I know we ⁷_____ have a great time AND make a lot of money!

See you there!

Mrs. Hendricks

14 Look at the students' schedule for next week. Complete the questions and answers with **am**/**is**/**are going to**.

CHILDREN HELPING – WEEKLY CALENDAR			
	Me	**Peter and Hugo**	**Sheila**
make a video of the music club	✓		
do a long walk for charity		✓	
sell tickets for the school play			✓

1 **A:** How _____ you _____ get children interested in joining the music club?

  B: I _____.

2 **A:** How _____ Peter and Hugo _____ raise money for charity?

  B: They _____.

3 **A:** What _____ Sheila _____ do next week?

  B: She _____.

Content Connection | Art

15 Match the words to the definitions. Write the letters.

____ 1 font   a pictures
____ 2 images   b the style of the letters
____ 3 design   c how the information is organized
____ 4 layout   d the way the font and images look
____ 5 effective   e successful

16 Listen and read. What does a successful ad need to have?

Effective Advertisements

Advertisements tell people about a product and make people want to buy it. Think of an ad that you think is effective. What makes it good? Is it the picture or is it the text? Maybe you like the way the images and font look or how the information is organized? A successful ad has an interesting design, images, and fonts. These things add to the impact of the ad. If the layout is good, the message is more effective. And, if the message is very effective, then it's a great ad!

A

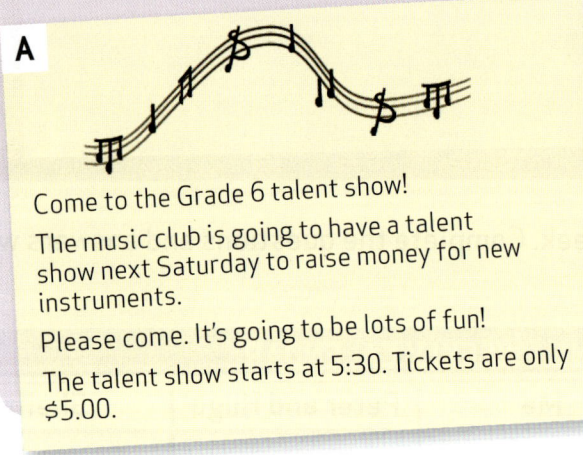

Come to the Grade 6 talent show!

The music club is going to have a talent show next Saturday to raise money for new instruments.

Please come. It's going to be lots of fun!

The talent show starts at 5:30. Tickets are only $5.00.

B

Come to the Grade 6 talent show!

We're raising money for new instruments.

Saturday evening.

Show starts at 5:30.

It's going to be lots of fun!

Tickets are only $5.00.

17 Look at the ads in **16**. Which one is more effective? Read and check **A** or **B**.

	A	B
1 The font is clear and easy to read.	☐	☐
2 The images tell me a lot about the talent show.	☐	☐
3 The layout is attractive.	☐	☐
4 The poster has an interesting design.	☐	☐
5 This poster makes me want to buy a ticket.	☐	☐
6 The information is clear and well organized.	☐	☐

18 Complete the sentences with the words in 15.

1 I like _____ of young children in advertisements because they make me feel happy.

2 If you use a clear _____ in your ad, then people will be able to read it more easily.

3 Effe planned the _____ of her poster carefully, thinking about where to put the writing and the pictures.

4 We think the advertisement about the shoes is _____ because it makes you want to wear them and dance!

5 That ad has a really attractive _____ – the images are colorful, and the font is modern.

THINK BIG

Design an effective advertisement for a talent show at your school.

Grammar

19 Read and circle.
1. I **have eaten** / **has eaten** chocolate pizza.
2. She **haven't baked** / **hasn't baked** bread before.
3. He **have ridden** / **has ridden** a bike to the top of a mountain.
4. **He's never been** / **He never has been** to Italy.
5. **You never have drunk** / **You haven't drunk** chocolate milk before.
6. We **haven't read** / **hasn't read** the Harry Potter books.

20 Read and match.

1. Have you ever watched a scary movie?
2. Has she ever baked cupcakes?
3. Have they ever been hiking?
4. Has he ever washed a car?

a. No, they haven't.
b. Yes, he has.
c. No, I haven't.
d. Yes, she has.

21 Complete the sentences. Use have or has with the correct form of the verb in parentheses.
1. We _____ (see) lions, elephants, and crocodiles in South Africa.
2. He _____ (ride) a horse many times on his grandparents' farm.
3. You _____ (make) a wonderful birthday card for your friend!
4. She _____ (write) an interesting story about life long ago.
5. They _____ (buy) a new vacation home.

22 Unscramble the sentences.

1 never / before / to / we've / Spain / been

_____

2 drawn / picture / big / hasn't / she / a

_____

3 never / they've / lake / a / in / swum / before

_____

4 I've / sung / talent / a / never / show / in

_____

5 bike / he's / a / ridden / before / never

_____

23 Write questions. Use **Have you ever …?**.

1 eat an insect

_____

2 play a guitar

_____

3 go rock climbing

_____

4 be on TV

_____

24 Now answer the questions in **23** for you.

1 _____
2 _____
3 _____
4 _____

Culture Connection | Around the World

25 Unscramble the words and write. Then match.

1 _____ netifeb
2 _____ esuac
3 _____ anetod
4 _____ esari
5 _____ retenulov

a to give something, like money, to an organization that needs help
b to offer to do something
c to collect money to help people
d to be helped by something
e an organization that people support

26 Read and complete. Then listen and check.

| benefit | cause | donate | raise | volunteer |

Companies That Help People

All over the world, there are many people that ¹_____ from the work of organizations and charities. You can help people in need, too, either by donating money to a good ²_____ or by working as a ³_____. You can also help ⁴_____ money for a charity or organization. Here are two companies that help people. Maybe you might want to ⁵_____ some money to one of them?

Child's Play
Being sick is no fun. Being sick in the hospital is terrible! You're alone, and you're scared. Your parents aren't there all the time. You don't have your computer, your video games, or any other games. People who worked at video game companies knew this and decided to help children in hospitals. They started a charity called Child's Play.

Child's Play gives laptops, video games, and video game consoles to hospitals. They also give toys and books. Sick children can enjoy them and feel better. Anyone can give money to Child's Play. It's a wonderful way to help children who are in the hospital.

Kiva
Kiva is a company that does what it can to help people. Kiva helps people start their own companies. For example, Josie is good at baking. She wants to start her own business and sell her delicious cookies and cakes. But it's expensive to start your own business, and Josie doesn't have a lot of money. Kiva can help. Kiva finds people that will lend Josie money to start her company. When her business becomes successful, she'll give the money back to the people that helped her. People can donate any amount of money to Kiva, even really small amounts. It's a great way to help others.

27 Read 26 again and circle.

1 Child's Play gives laptops and video games to ____.
  a children
  b hospitals

2 The people who started Child's Play worked ____.
  a in hospitals
  b at video game companies

3 Kiva helps people who want to ____.
  a start a company
  b make cookies and cakes

4 Kiva helps people find ____.
  a people who need money
  b people who will lend money

28 Complete the sentences with the words from the box.

> amount   charity   company   delicious   lend

1 In my city, there is a _____ that gives soup and bread to homeless people for lunch.
2 Mehmet baked _____ cupcakes and sold them for 50¢ each.
3 My grandfather donates a large _____ of money every year.
4 In London, there's a _____ that helps people study and get better jobs.
5 The organization will _____ you money to help you start a business.

THINK BIG

How about you? Answer the question.

You have $100 to donate to charity. Which of the charities in 26 do you want to help? Why?

_____
_____
_____
_____

Unit 3 43

Writing | Letter

A well-written letter is well organized and contains clear ideas. It usually includes:

- the date
- a greeting, such as *Dear Mr. Smith,*
- the body of the letter
- a closing, such as *Sincerely,* or *Best wishes,*
- your signature (your name)

The letter in this unit offers suggestions. When you write a letter that gives a suggestion, the body of the letter includes:

- your idea or suggestion
- how people can carry out the idea
- why the idea is important

29 Write the parts of the letter.

> body   closing   date   greeting   signature

1 _____ May 10, 2014

2 _____ Dear Mr. Green,

3 _____ I think that the school should raise money to help the *Houses for All* charity. This charity builds homes for homeless families. We could raise money for this charity. We could collect coins and raise money that way or we could organize cake sales to raise money.

This project is a good one because all children deserve a good home. We can help. Please think about this idea.

4 _____ Sincerely,

5 _____ Teresa Lee

30 Look at 29. Circle the answers in the letter.

What's the suggestion?

How can people carry out the idea?

Why is the idea important?

31 Write a letter to your teacher. Suggest a plan to raise money for a charity.

44 Unit 3

Review

32 How can these students raise money at their school fair? Write suggestions with could.

I'm Maria. I have a lot of books, but I don't need them.

I'm Fred. I'm really good at painting T-shirts.

I'm Eric. I have a video camera, and I enjoy making videos.

I'm Gaby. I really enjoy writing.

1 Maria _____.
2 Fred _____.
3 Eric _____.
4 Gaby _____.

33 Complete the sentences. Use am/is/are going to.

A: How ¹_____ we ²_____ raise money for computers at school?

B: I have a plan. We ³_____ organize a contest.

A: And how ⁴_____ you ⁵_____ tell people about the contest?

B: I ⁶_____ make big posters and put them up all over school.

A: How ⁷_____ the contest ⁸_____ help raise money?

B: Maybe we could ask students to buy a ticket to be in the contest.

A: Well, I don't know… What kind of contest ⁹_____ you ¹⁰_____ have?

B: We ¹¹_____ have an online writing contest. Children can write a paragraph titled: *Why we need computers at school*. That's a great idea, isn't it?

A: That's silly! The school doesn't have computers! Children can't write online.

B: Oh. OK.

Unit 3 **45**

Checkpoint | Units 1–3

1 Look at the pictures. Write the words. Add your own words on the extra line.

MY INTERESTS
1 _____
2 _____
3 _____
4 _____
5 _____

FAMILY TIES
1 _____
2 _____
3 _____
4 _____
5 _____

HELPING OTHERS
1 _____
2 _____
3 _____
4 _____
5 _____

46 Checkpoint Units 1–3

2 Think of a famous person or a cartoon character. Complete the information about him or her.

Name _____	
Interests	He or she is interested in: _____ He or she is good at: _____ He or she likes: _____
Family Ties	Here are some family events in his or her life: _____ _____ _____
Helping Others	Here's a way he or she could help: _____ _____ Here's what he or she is going to do: _____ _____

3 Think about a song your person could like. Use **1** and **2** to help you. Choose a song and write a letter to your person about it. Explain why you chose this song.

Checkpoint Units 1–3 **47**

unit 4
SHOPPING AROUND

1 Match the pictures to the places. Write the numbers.

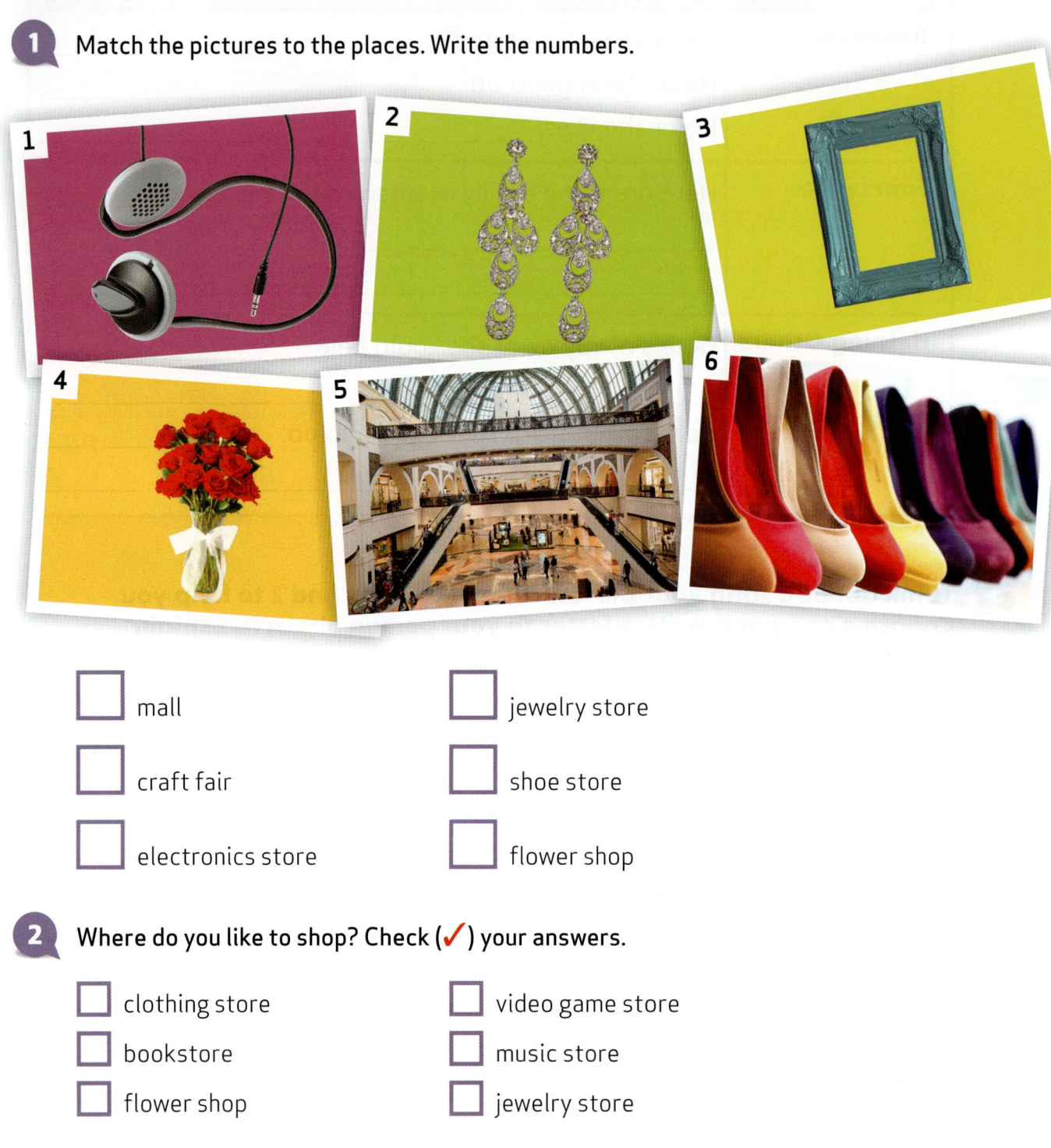

- [ ] mall
- [ ] craft fair
- [ ] electronics store
- [ ] jewelry store
- [ ] shoe store
- [ ] flower shop

2 Where do you like to shop? Check (✓) your answers.

- [ ] clothing store
- [ ] bookstore
- [ ] flower shop
- [ ] video game store
- [ ] music store
- [ ] jewelry store

3 Look at 1. Which of these places are there in your neighborhood? Circle them.

4 Listen and number the pictures.

5 Where could you buy these presents? Circle the correct answers.

1 a turquoise necklace
   a a craft fair   b an electronics store

2 silver earrings
   a a flower shop   b a jewelry store

3 a beaded bracelet
   a a mall   b a music store

4 balloons
   a a mall   b a craft fair

5 roses
   a a bookstore   b a flower shop

6 a handmade picture frame
   a a craft fair   b a sports store

Think about some presents for your family.

Your sister loves jewelry. What kind of jewelry could you buy her for her birthday? _____

Your mom loves flowers. What kind of flowers could you buy her for Mother's Day? _____

Your dad likes handmade things from craft fairs. What could you buy him for Father's Day? _____

Unit 4

Reading | Product reviews

 6 Listen and read. Then ✓ the correct person.

- ▶ Gadgets
- ▶ Music
- ▶ Games & Puzzles
- ▶ Books
- ▼ Remote control
  - • Cars and Trucks
  - • Planes, Helicopters, Boats
  - • Robots

KIDS RULE:
KIDS TELLING IT LIKE IT IS

Click on any category. Come on, kids! Write a review.

THE RC SUPER SPEEDO RACER
$55.00
Average Rating ★★★

By Cowgirl (Sydney, Australia)
★★★★

I LOVE this car! It's powerful and runs really well on the wood floors in my room! It crashes into walls and bounces right off! It's expensive, but a lot of fun. It's as exciting as the most expensive remote control cars. Actually, I think it's even more fun!

By Tomcat (Canterbury, England)
★★

Not great. Not as much fun as the KoolKat Kar. The KoolKat Kar runs very fast on concrete floors and even on carpets. The RC Super Speedo Racer doesn't have a lot of power. It can't even race on carpets. The RC Super Speedo Racer is less expensive, but for a few dollars more you can get the KoolKat Kar and have a lot more fun!

	Cowgirl	Tomcat
1 Who likes the RC Super Speedo Racer?	☐	☐
2 Who thinks the RC Super Speedo Racer isn't powerful?	☐	☐
3 Who thinks the RC Super Speedo Racer is less exciting than the more expensive remote cars?	☐	☐
4 Who thinks the RC Super Speedo Racer is expensive?	☐	☐
5 Who likes racing powerful cars that can race on carpets?	☐	☐

7 Answer the question.

Which car would you like to buy: The RC Super Speedo Racer or the KoolKat Kar? Why?

Language in Action

8 Listen. Then answer the questions.

Jen: How about this one? It got some really great reviews. Look.

Eddie: Oh, yes? Is it as nice as yours?

Jen: Definitely. It's a really good player, and it's the least expensive one in the store.

Eddie: Yeah, but it's $85! I don't have that much money.

Jen: Yes, but look. It's on sale! Let's see, it's only $60. It has four gigabytes of memory. And it comes with a free case.

Eddie: Wow! I really like the design, too. It's perfect! There's only one problem.

Jen: What?

Eddie: It's already sold out.

Jen: You're joking!

1 Who knows more about MP3 players, Jen or Eddie? _____

2 Does Eddie need to buy a case for the MP3 player? _____

3 Why doesn't Eddie buy the MP3 player? _____

9 Look at 8. Read the underlined expressions. How can you say them in other words? Match and write the letter.

____ 1 How about…?   a I'm really disappointed!
____ 2 Oh, yes?   b I know but…
____ 3 Definitely.   c What do you think of…?
____ 4 Yeah, but   d Really?
____ 5 You're joking!   e Yes.

10 Complete the dialog with the expressions in 9.

A: ¹_____ going to the craft fair? There's a big one today.

B: ²_____ Where is it?

A: It's in the park, near school.

B: Great. Maybe I can get a birthday present for my brother.

A: ³_____

B: Hey, did you feel that? It's raining!

A: ⁴_____ Now we can't go!

Language in Action

> The blue shoes are **expensive**.
> The red shoes are **more expensive than** the blue shoes.
> The black shoes are **the most expensive** of all.
> The red shoes are not **as expensive as** the black shoes.
>
> The white shoes are **less expensive than** the blue shoes.
> The white shoes are **the least expensive** of all.

11 Look at the ratings. Circle the correct answers.

Movie Reviews
Category: Sci Fi

The Story	Horrible ★	Boring ★★	OK ★★★	Interesting ★★★★	Amazing ★★★★★
The Acting	Terrible ★	Disappointing ★★	OK ★★★	Very Good ★★★★	Extraordinary ★★★★★
Popularity	Flop ★	Not Popular ★★	OK ★★★	Very Popular ★★★★	Extremely Popular ★★★★★

	Story	Acting	Popularity
Robots of the Universe	★★★★★	★★	★★★★
Princess of Evil	★★★★	★★★	★★★★★
The Pirates	★	★★★★★	★★★

1 *The Pirates* is **less / more** popular than *Princess of Evil*.
2 The story of *Princess of Evil* is **less / more** interesting than the story of *The Pirates*.
3 The acting in *Princess of Evil* is **less / more** extraordinary than the acting in *Robots of the Universe*.
4 *The Pirates* is **the most / the least** popular movie.
5 The story of *Robots of the Universe* is **the least / the most** amazing.
6 *Princess of Evil* is **the most / the least** popular movie.

12 Look at the ratings in **11**. Then complete the sentences with more/less ... than or the most/the least.

1 The story of *Robots of the Universe* is _____ amazing _____ the story of *Princess of Evil*.
2 The acting in *Robots of the Universe* is _____ extraordinary of all the movies.
3 The story in *The Pirates* is _____ boring of all.
4 The story in *The Pirates* is _____ interesting _____ the story in the other two movies.

52 Unit 4

Language in Action

13 Complete the sentences. Use *as ... as* or *not as ... as* and the words in parentheses.

1. The black jeans are _____ the blue jeans. (fashionable)
2. The black jeans are _____ the blue jeans. (cheap)
3. The blue jeans are _____ the black jeans. (baggy)
4. The black jeans are _____ the blue jeans. (popular)
5. The blue jeans are _____ the black jeans. (comfortable)

The price of those sneakers is **too** high.	The price isn't low **enough**.
Those jeans are **too** baggy.	The jeans aren't tight **enough**.

14 Look at **13**. Circle the correct answers.

1. My brother wears really baggy jeans. The blue jeans _____ for him.
   a aren't baggy enough   b are too baggy
2. I like colorful pants. Those jeans _____ for me.
   a aren't colorful enough   b are too colorful
3. I usually wear white sweaters with my jeans. That sweater _____ for me.
   a isn't bright enough   b is too bright
4. We never buy jeans that are too expensive. These jeans are perfect. The price _____.
   a is cheap enough   b is too cheap

Content Connection | History

15 Read and complete the puzzle with the words from the box.

coins
livestock
metal
paper
shells
trade

ACROSS
3 Exchange one thing for another
5 Cows and goats
6 Round metal money

DOWN
1 Bank notes are made of this.
2 This is very shiny – silver is one type of this.
4 Some animals live in these.

16 Listen and read. Who used the first paper money?

The Idea for Paper Money

1 Long ago, people didn't use bank cards, paper money, or coins to buy things. They bartered with livestock and grain, exchanging them for the things they needed. Over time, people started using other things as money, such as cowrie shells. They exchanged the shells for food, animals, and other goods. Then metal coins were made and, finally, paper money. The story of paper money is a fascinating one. The use of bank notes started in the Tang Dynasty. The Tang Dynasty existed in China from AD 618–907.

2 Before Chinese people used paper money, they used coins. The coins were round and had a square hole in the middle. They kept their coins on a rope, so the more coins they had on the rope, the heavier the rope would be. Rich people found that their ropes of coins were too heavy to carry around easily. So what did they do? They left their strings of coins with someone they trusted, and that person wrote down the amount of money he was keeping for them on a piece of paper and gave it to them. When the rich man wanted his money, he took the piece of paper to that trusted person, and he got his coins back. This was a good idea, don't you think? Eventually, paper bank notes were created, and people began to use them instead of ropes of coins.

54 Unit 4

17 Read **16** again and answer the questions.

1 What did people barter with long ago?
   _____

2 What was used as money before coins were made?
   _____

3 How did Chinese people keep money long ago?
   _____

4 What did rich people do with their coin ropes when they were too heavy?
   _____

5 What did that trusted person give the coin owner?
   _____

18 Read and ✓.

1 to trade goods for other goods, rather than for money
   a barter ☐   b keep ☐

2 to give something to someone and get something back from them
   a exist ☐   b exchange ☐

3 lived
   a traded ☐   b existed ☐

4 someone you believe to be honest and reliable
   a trusted ☐   b rich ☐

5 very interesting
   a good ☐   b fascinating ☐

THINK BIG

What's the best way to pay for these things – coins, bank notes, or credit card?

Newspaper	
Pair of designer jeans	
Laptop computer	
Plane tickets	

Unit 4 55

Grammar

19 Read and circle.

1. This bracelet is cheaper than that **one** / **ones**.
2. These shoes are more expensive than those **one** / **ones**.
3. I like the silver earrings more than the beaded **one** / **ones**.
4. Those balloons are more colorful than these **one** / **ones**.
5. That pair of jeans looks bigger than this **one** / **ones**.
6. My favorite necklace is the turquoise **one** / **ones**.
7. That model of camera is more interesting than this **one** / **ones**.

20 Read and match.

1. Could you help me, please?
2. What size is this?
3. What's it made of?
4. How much is it?
5. Would you like to try it on?

a. It's a size 8.
b. It's made of cotton.
c. Yes, please.
d. Of course. What would you like?
e. It's $10.49.

21 Complete the sentences with the words from the box.

| help | model | made | much | ones | pair | size |

1. Would you like to try on the black jeans or the other _____?
2. How _____ is the bunch of red roses?
3. These shoes are too small. Do you have a bigger _____?
4. Hello. Can I _____ you?
5. Which _____ is the silver camera in the window?
6. Do you have this _____ of pants in a size 12, please?
7. Excuse me, what's this bag _____ of? Is it leather?

56 Unit 4

22 Put the sentences in order to make a dialog. Write the numbers.

a _____ Can I help you?

b _____ It's $49.99. Would you like to take it?

c _____ Yes, please. I'm looking for a new watch.

d _____ It's made of real leather. Would you like to try it on?

e _____ Oh, yes. I'll take it. Thank you!

f _____ How about this one? We have it in black and in brown.

g _____ Yes, please. Oh, look, it fits perfectly! How much is it?

h _____ Hmm, I like the black one. What's it made of?

23 Read the answers and write the questions.

1 _____
Yes, please. I'm looking for a jacket.

2 _____
It's a size 12.

3 _____
It's $34.99.

4 _____
It's made of cotton.

5 _____
It's the new model.

6 _____
No, thank you, I won't take it.

Unit 4 57

Culture Connection | Around the World

24 Read and ✓.

1. vendor
   - a someone who buys something
   - b someone who sells something
2. browse
   - a to look at things without buying
   - b to look at things and buy them
3. haggle
   - a to argue about the price
   - b to agree about the price
4. experience
   - a something that you feel
   - b something that happens to you
5. features
   - a important parts
   - b important things

25 Listen and read. Why is bargaining a good skill in some places?

Shopping Is Fun!

Not everyone enjoys shopping. But, for those that do enjoy it, there are different shopping experiences around the world. Some people like to haggle and buy things for the cheapest price. Others just like to browse and not buy anything. For some, shopping is the chance to dress up as a character when they visit their favorite store. Read more about two very different shopping experiences in the world.

How to shop in Chatuchak Market, Bangkok

Chatuchak Market is a great place to bargain. Everyone bargains here. When you bargain, you try to pay a lower price for something. Here's an example. You want to buy a hat. The hat costs $20. You say to the vendor, the person who sells the hat, "I want to pay $10." The vendor says, "That's too cheap. How about $15?" You say, "Definitely not! That's still too expensive. How about $12?" The vendor says, "OK, $12." Because you bargained, you just paid $8 less for the hat!

Bargaining is a good skill to have when you shop in some places. You can buy things for less money, and this means you can buy more things.

Mandarake in Akihabara, Tokyo

The most popular place in Akihabara could be Mandarake. This is the largest manga and anime store in the world. The store includes all eight floors in a building. It's full of DVDs of anime movies, comic books, and action figures of your favorite characters. The customers who shop at Akihabara are very interesting, too. Some of them dress up to look like the characters in animation movies, like Sailor Moon, Pokemon, and Super Mario. These people wear costumes and make-up and really enjoy acting like their favorite characters.

26 Read 25 again and circle **T** for true and **F** for false.

1	Everyone loves to shop.	T	F
2	When you browse, you don't buy anything.	T	F
3	You can bargain at Chatuchak Market.	T	F
4	When you bargain, you want to pay more for something.	T	F
5	Mandarake is the largest manga and anime store in the world.	T	F
6	Some customers at Mandarake dress up as sports heroes.	T	F

27 Find and write the words from 24.

1 _____ glegah
2 _____ wesrob
3 _____ rdonve
4 _____ sreuatef
5 _____ xerepneiec

THINK BIG

Can you bargain? Complete the dialog.

You: How much is the bag?
Vendor: It's $25.
You: _____
_____
Vendor: How about $20?
You: _____
_____
Vendor: You can have it for $15. OK?
You: _____
_____
Vendor: Alright then. $12.50. Just for you.

Unit 4 **59**

Writing | Product review

A good product review describes what is good and bad about a product and gives a recommendation. A recommendation tells the readers if they should buy the product.

Here are ways to say if a product is good or bad:

Good
It's the best.
They're worth the money.
It's great.

Bad
It's terrible.
They're not worth the money.
It isn't great.

Here are ways to give a recommendation:

I definitely recommend this product.
This product isn't great but [say why some people might like it].
I don't recommend this product because…

Remember to explain your ideas.

28 Read the product review. Answer the questions. Write the sentence numbers.

¹I bought my Wrap-Arounds at Cheap Charlie. ²They aren't great headphones, but they're good for people who don't have a lot of money. ³You can buy more expensive headphones and get more amazing sound, but why? ⁴I think they're worth the money, especially if you don't need to hear extraordinary sound. ⁵I recommend Wrap-Arounds because they offer good sound for little money.

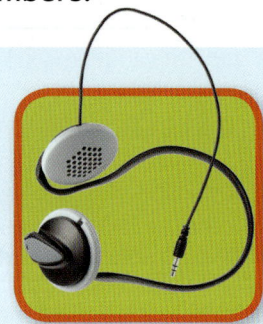

Which sentence explains…

1 who would like the headphones?

2 why the headphones are worth the money?

3 if you should buy the headphones?

29 Choose a gadget you have or want. Write a review.

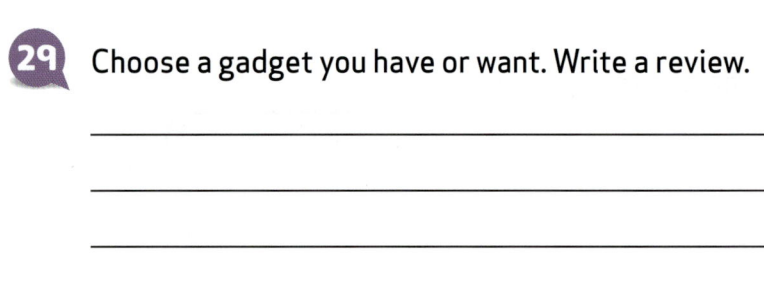

TIPS

To write a good review you need to decide these things:

1 Do you like the product or not? Why/Why not?

2 What's good or bad about it?

3 Is it worth the money?

4 Will you recommend it or not?

Review

30 Write the words in the correct column.

> bracelet   clothing store   craft fair   digital camera   earrings
> flower shop   headphones   MP3 player   necklace

Jewelry	Gadgets	Places
_____	_____	_____
_____	_____	_____
_____	_____	_____

31 Look at the ratings. Complete the sentences. Write more/less popular than and the most/the least popular.

★★★★★   ★★★   ★★★★

1. The turquoise necklace is _____ the beaded one.
2. The beaded bracelet is _____ the silver earrings.
3. The turquoise necklace is _____ of them all.
4. The beaded bracelet is _____ of them all.

32 Write the sentences. Use too or not … enough and the words in parentheses.

1. These shoes look like boats on my feet. They're _____. (big)
2. This digital camera costs a lot of money. It's _____. (expensive)
3. I can't hear the video. It's _____. (loud)
4. These headphones always break. They're _____ (strong).

Unit 4   61

unit 5
VACATION TIME

1 Which vacations do you see in the pictures? Write the numbers.

- ☐ riding a bike in the forest
- ☐ snorkeling on a coral reef
- ☐ lying on the beach
- ☐ hiking in the mountains
- ☐ kayaking down a river
- ☐ skiing in the snow
- ☐ doing water sports on a lake
- ☐ visiting an amusement park

2 Look at 1. Which vacation would you like the best? Which vacation would you like the least? Rank the vacations and write their numbers in the chart.

The least				The most
👍	👍👍	👍👍👍	👍👍👍👍	👍👍👍👍👍

3 Write the words in the correct rows.

> a helmet   a life jacket   a map   a warm jacket   a water bottle
> a windbreaker   insect repellent   sunglasses   sunscreen

useful clothing	
useful for eyes	
useful for skin	
useful for safety/health	

4 Look at 3. Complete the sentences.

1 I'm wearing _____ because there are a lot of insects in the woods.
2 Take _____. You'll get thirsty on the hike.
3 When you go horseback riding, wear _____. You could fall.
4 I'm glad we took _____ on our bike trip. We almost got lost.
5 It was very cold in the mountains, so I wore _____.
6 The captain of the boat gave me _____ because the water was rough and dangerous.
7 I didn't put on enough _____ at the beach, and now I have a sunburn.
8 When you walk on the beach in the winter, it can be windy and wet. Be sure to wear _____.

I'm going to go biking on a forest path on a very sunny day. It's sometimes windy in the afternoons. What should I take to be comfortable and safe?

THINK BIG

_____, _____, _____,

_____, _____

_____, and _____

Reading | Narrative story

 Listen and read. Then answer the questions.

A Family's Kayaking Trip

Joe felt awful when he woke up. His head hurt. His stomach hurt. His ears hurt. He was sad because his family was going kayaking soon. His mom looked at him and said, "Sorry, Joe, you're too sick to go with us. You're going to stay at home with Grandma." Joe was angry! It wasn't fair!

His family said goodbye and left. Joe was staring at the TV when his grandma came in. She said, "Don't worry, Joe. You'll go kayaking another day."

Joe stared at the ceiling. He was thinking about his family. They were probably having a wonderful time. He closed his eyes and pictured them. They were in their kayaks on the river, laughing and having fun. There were deer and rabbits on the river banks and birds everywhere.

He was sleeping when his family returned. He woke up as they came into his room. They looked miserable. His mom said, "We had a terrible time. We all got mosquito bites. I fell and hurt my arm on the way to the river. Your sister fell into the river when she got out of her kayak. Your dad hit his head on a tree branch hanging over the river. You're very lucky that you stayed at home."

1 What did Joe's family do?
_____

2 Why didn't Joe go with his family?
_____

3 How did Joe imagine his family's day?
_____

4 Why was Joe surprised when he saw his family?
_____

6 Answer the questions. Explain your answers.

1 Do you think Joe still wants to go kayaking?
_____

2 Do you think his family wants to go kayaking again?
_____

3 Do you want to go kayaking?
_____

Language in Action

7 Listen. Then circle the correct answers.

Eve: So how did your vacation go?

Gina: It was terrible. On the second day, we went shopping in a small town. I was excited at first. One store had nice souvenirs. You know, T-shirts and magnets, stuff like that.

Eve: I bet you got something wonderful.

Gina: Well, I had my eye on a really beautiful pair of earrings. But while I was shopping, I lost my purse. By the time I found it, all the stores were closed!

Eve: Aw, that's a shame. But I guess you saved a lot of money that way!

Gina: Ha, ha! Very funny!

1. Did Gina have a good time?
   a Yes, she did.
   b No, she didn't.

2. Did Gina really think Eve was funny?
   a Yes, she did.
   b No, she didn't.

8 Look at 7. Read the underlined expressions. Think about the meaning. Then circle the correct answers.

1. Eve asks, "How did your vacation go?" What does she want to know?
   a how Gina traveled while on vacation
   b whether Gina enjoyed her vacation

2. What other "stuff like that" can you buy at a souvenir shop?
   a postcards, tourist books, and maps
   b ovens, refrigerators, and desks

3. What does Eve mean when she says, "I bet"?
   a I think.
   b I know.

4. Gina "had her eye on" a pair of earrings. What did she want to do?
   a She wanted to buy them.
   b She looked at them closely.

5. When Eve says, "a shame," what does she mean?
   a I'm sorry you didn't feel well.
   b I'm sorry the stores were closed.

9 Complete the dialog with the expressions in 8.

A: Last week, I went to a great street market in Corsica. I ¹_____ some beautiful scarves there. ²_____ you'd like them. They were your favorite colors.

B: What else did they have?

A: Local food and desserts, traditional pottery… ³_____. It was all amazing!

Unit 5 **65**

Language in Action

What **was** he **doing** when he got hurt?	He **was riding** a horse when he got hurt.
What happened while they **were hiking**?	They got lost while they **were hiking**.

10 Find and circle the four verbs in the iguana's tail. Use the verbs to answer the question.

Itbiawasridingduowassurfingintwaswalkingiwasclimbinglu

What was the iguana doing when it got hurt? It:

1 _____ 2 _____
3 _____ 4 _____

11 Match the two parts of the sentences. Write the letters.

____ 1 While Jack was hiking in the snowy mountains, …   a he got lost and very cold.

____ 2 Sue and Ben sang songs…   b when he rode into a tree.

____ 3 Steve was riding his bicycle…   c they realized they didn't have the plane tickets!

____ 4 When Jim and his mom were driving to the airport, …   d while they were kayaking down the river.

12 Look at **11**. Answer the questions.

1 What was Jack doing when he got lost in the mountains? _____
   _____

2 What happened while Sue and Ben were singing? _____
   _____

3 What was Steve doing when he hit a tree? _____
   _____

Language in Action

Was he riding his bike when it started to rain?	Yes, he was./No, he wasn't.
Were you swimming when you got sunburned?	Yes, I was./No, I wasn't.

13 Complete the questions with the correct form of wear. Then write the answers.

1 _____ sunglasses when you saw him on the beach?

_____

2 _____ life jackets when they got splashed by a wave?

_____

3 _____ a warm jacket when she climbed up Greenfell Mountain?

_____

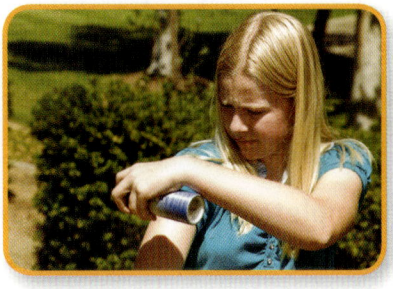

4 _____ insect repellent when you saw her?

_____

5 _____ a helmet when he fell off his bike?

_____

6 _____ sunscreen when you saw her at the beach?

_____

Unit 5 67

Content Connection | Math

14 Read and ✓.

1 to add numbers together
   a multiplication ☐   b addition ☐

2 someone who buys things
   a customer ☐   b receipt ☐

3 something you buy
   a item ☐   b price ☐

4 to add the same number several times
   a addition ☐   b multiplication ☐

5 a list of what things cost
   a souvenir ☐   b price list ☐

6 to help customers in a store
   a serve ☐   b sell ☐

7 a piece of paper showing you've paid for something
   a gift ☐   b receipt ☐

8 an object you keep to remind you of a particular place
   a gift ☐   b souvenir ☐

15 Read and complete with the words from the box. Then listen and check.

| chips   customers   items   multiplication   price list   sunburned   sunscreen   water |

Jim's Problem

One day, Jim was lying on the beach when he realized he was ¹_____. He was also hungry and thirsty. So he went to Beach Shack. He looked at the ²_____ to see what to buy. He picked up five ³_____: three bags of ⁴_____, a bottle of ⁵_____, and some ⁶_____. But when Jim went to pay, the girl who was serving the ⁷_____ said, "That's $11.51, please." Oh, no! Jim didn't have enough money! He wasn't very good at addition and ⁸_____. He solved his problem by putting back two bags of chips.

How about you? How would you solve the problem?

68 Unit 5

16 Read **15** again and circle.

1 How much more money did Jim need?
He needed **$11.51 / $2.18**.

2 How did Jim solve his problem?
He bought **one bag of chips / a bottle of water**.

3 How many items did Jim buy?
He bought **five items / three items**.

4 What math did Jim use to find the totals?
He used **addition only / addition and multiplication**.

17 Complete the sentences with some of the words in **14**. Then do the sums.

1 A _____ buys four apples for 35¢ each. How much does he pay altogether?

2 Daphne buys a _____ for $3.75, insect repellent for $3.15, and three postcards for 65¢ each. How much does she pay altogether?

3 On the _____ it says 85¢ for a bottle of water. If you have $5.00, how many bottles of water can you buy?

4 Mr. Arzul _____ about twenty-eight customers a day in his small gift shop. About how many customers does he serve in three days?

THINK BIG

Write about how you would solve Jim's problem.

_____
_____
_____
_____

Grammar

18 Read and circle.
1 **What / Which** were you doing at school last night?
2 **Why / Who** was going to the park yesterday?
3 **When / Where** was the bus leaving?
4 **What / Why** were they talking so loudly?
5 **Where / When** were the children running to?
6 **Which / Why** bag was she carrying?

19 Read and match.

1 Where was he going on his bike?   a He was flying his kite.

2 Why were they wearing lifejackets?   b Because she was thirsty.

3 What was he doing on the beach?   c He was going to the park.

4 Why was she drinking water?   d Because they were rafting.

20 Complete the sentences. Use **was** or **were**.
1 When _____ the dog barking?
2 Why _____ she swimming in the rain?
3 Who _____ shouting in the street last night?
4 What _____ you watching on TV?
5 Where _____ they going for a vacation?

21 Unscramble and write the questions.

1 what / doing / was / he broke / his leg / when / he

   _____

2 was / who / on the phone / talking to / she

   _____

3 they / were / when / from Europe / coming back

   _____

4 singing / you / where / so beautifully / were

   _____

5 was / why / shouting at / your brother / you

   _____

22 Answer the questions in **21** using full sentences.

1 climbing a mountain

   _____

2 her friend

   _____

3 in the winter

   _____

4 at the concert

   _____

5 because I was noisy

   _____

23 Answer these questions for you.

1 What were you doing last night?

   _____

2 Who were you talking to this morning?

   _____

3 Where were you going yesterday?

   _____

Unit 5 71

Culture Connection | Around the World

24 Match the words to the definitions. Write the letters.

____ 1 expedition   a very interesting
____ 2 guide   b the area around the North Pole
____ 3 arctic   c especially
____ 4 fascinating   d a trip around a place with a guide
____ 5 particularly   e someone whose job is to show a place to tourists
____ 6 guided tour   f a long trip that is carefully planned

25 Listen and read. Match headings A–E to paragraphs 1–5.

A Different Types of Family Vacations ____
B Cultural Activities on a Staycation ____
C Going on a Staycation ____
D Advantages of a Staycation ____
E Example of a Staycation ____

A Staycation in Italy

1 Every year, families all over the world go on vacation. Vacations are wonderful times to be with family and explore new places and cultures. Many families like visiting other countries while on vacation and learning about the history of a particular country from guides. Other families enjoy discovering parts of their own country and learning more about their own history and culture. Sometimes families like to stay at home. They don't like to travel, but they do like to explore new places and cultures. How can they do both? These families can go on a "staycation."

2 Here is how a staycation works. Your family decides on a culture and a country that they want to know more about. They do research and find out about that country's music, crafts, food, art, and other things. Then they try to create the culture in their home during the vacation.

3 For example, say that your family wants to learn more about Italian culture. Your family would do research and find out about the following things:
 • popular Italian food   • Italian art
 • popular Italian music   • Italian vacations and other events
 • popular Italian stories   • the Italian language

4 During the staycation, your family would plan activities to do together to learn about Italian culture. You might eat at Italian restaurants, go on a guided tour at a museum to study Italian artists, and see Italian movies.

5 Staycations are a great way to enjoy your family, stay at home, and learn fascinating things, too!

26 Read **25** again and correct the sentences.

1. On a staycation, families stay at homes around the world.
   _____

2. Families who go on a staycation are not interested in learning about other places and cultures.
   _____

3. A family on an Italian staycation could eat French food, watch American movies, and learn German.
   _____

4. Staycations are great for a family that wants to get away and learn about the world.
   _____

27 Complete the sentences with the words from the box.

> crafts   culture   discovering   events   explore

1. At the market, you can buy _____ from many different countries.
2. Some families enjoy _____ new places when they go on vacation.
3. It's fun to see how other countries celebrate birthdays and other special _____.
4. Many people love learning about the history and _____ of another country.
5. Some families like to have a guided tour of a new place while others like to _____ on their own.

THINK BIG

Imagine your family is going on a staycation. What culture would you like to learn about?
_____

What are two things you would like to learn about that culture?
_____
_____

Unit 5

Writing | Postcards

Writing postcards is a great way to share your vacation with friends and family. Choose a postcard with a picture of a place you visited or plan on visiting. On the other side, there is a space for the address of the person you are writing to and a space for a short note about the picture or your trip. A postcard includes in this order:

- the **date** (*July 5th*)
- a **greeting** (*Hi* or *Dear* ...)
- a **body** with information about the place or your plans (*I'm having a great time! We went to the beach yesterday.*)
- a **closing** (*See you soon!* or *I miss you!*)

Don't forget to sign your name. You want your friends and family to know the postcard comes from you! And on the right side of the card, don't forget to put the full address of the person you are writing to (name, street address, town/city, postcode, country).

28 Write the parts of the postcard.

1 _____ See you soon!
2 _____ Dear Aunt Edna,
3 _____ August 22nd
4 _____ I'm so happy. I'm having a wonderful time with my family in South Africa. The weather's warm. The animals in the safari park were amazing. Tomorrow we're going to Cape Town.

29 Imagine you are visiting a place you know well. Answer these questions.

What's the name of the place? _____
What are you doing there? _____
What exciting things have you seen? _____
Are you enjoying yourself? Why/Why not? _____
What's your teacher's address at school? _____

30 Use your answers in **29**. Write a postcard to your teacher about that place.

Which one doesn't belong? Why?

letter / postcard / email

_____

74 Unit 5

Review

31 Find and circle the words. Then write the words in the correct columns.

> biking   campsite   helmet   rafting   skiing   tent

```
c s d x d g d v m c
r a f t i n g r e k
n g m t f a s g k u
g o t p l k i n g n
e b l o s k i n g
u i g t u i g l d i
l k o i f g t e n t
t i i h e l m e t g
o n w r i t i n g a
n g a e n t t g i t
r c f o i a s f n o
```

Vacation activities

_____

_____

_____

Vacation things

_____

_____

_____

32 Complete the sentences. Use the correct form of the words from the box.

> driving   looking   putting on   reading

1 We _____ to the amusement park when it started to rain.

2 My dad _____ at a map when he saw the snake right in front of him!

3 My mom got sunburned while she _____ her book on the beach.

4 I _____ sunscreen when I got stung by a bee.

33 Read. Then answer the questions.

> Yesterday morning, Tim and Jill were swimming in the lake because it was hot. Yesterday afternoon, Jill went hiking while Tim was at a picnic.

1 Was Tim hiking yesterday morning?

_____

2 Was Jill hiking yesterday afternoon?

_____

3 Why were Tim and Jill swimming in the lake yesterday?

_____

Unit 5

unit 6
THE FUTURE

1 Which of these inventions do you think will be common in stores by 2020? Check (✓) your answers.

- ☐ 3D video games
- ☐ Moon Cruiser
- ☐ Fly Car
- ☐ Chameleon Clothes
- ☐ Robot Help

2 Look at **1**. Which inventions would you like to buy? Circle the numbers.

1   2   3   4   5

76   Unit 6

3 What can you do with these electronic devices? Check (✓) your answers.

You can...	smartphone	MP3 player	tablet	laptop computer
1 Make phone calls				
2 Write essays and do homework				
3 Listen to music				
4 Watch movies and play games				
5 Text people				

4 Unscramble the words. Use the words in 3.

1 She listens to music on her _____.   3PM lpyrae
2 They read stories on their _____.   ptmsrahneo
3 He watches movies on his _____.   taetbl
4 He does his homework on his _____.   ptlopa mopetcur

Which electronic device is most useful for doing homework? Why?

_____

Which electronic device is best for playing games? Why?

_____

Unit 6 77

Reading | Science fiction

 5 Listen and read. Then answer the questions.

Jenny's Bad Morning

Jenny, a Grade 6 student, was sleeping when her bed started shaking. While the bed was shaking, a strange voice said, "Jenny, wake up! Time to go to school!" "You'll wake everybody up! Stop shaking and talking!" Jenny said. "Sorry," said the bed.

"I'm hungry," said Jenny. "Good morning, Jenny," a robot chair said. She sat on the robot and patted it. The robot carried her to the kitchen. "What would you like for breakfast, Jenny?" asked the fridge.

Jenny said, "Crunchy Crisp Cereal and toast, please." Five seconds later, the fridge opened up and put a bowl of cold cereal in front of her, and the toaster added hot toast with butter.

After breakfast, Jenny sat on the robot chair again, and it took her to her room. Jenny got dressed. "These clothes are too tight," said Jenny. The robot said, "Clothes, be bigger." The clothes got a little bigger. "Perfect!" said Jenny.

It was time for school. Jenny's mom said, "Hurry up, Jenny, get in the Fly Car." "Fly Car? No one rides in Fly Cars anymore," thought Jenny. Jenny wanted to use a Flying Suit to fly her to school. Her mom shook her head. "Sorry, you can't use a Flying Suit until you're 12." Jenny got in the Fly Car. She wasn't happy. She hated being 11! She thought, "I want to be 12! It'll be so much more fun."

1 How does Jenny wake up?

_____

2 Who makes Jenny's breakfast?

_____

3 How does Jenny get to school?

_____

4 Does Jenny like the Fly Car? Why/Why not?

_____

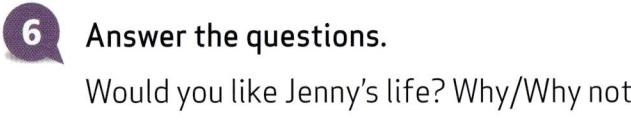 **6** Answer the questions.

Would you like Jenny's life? Why/Why not?

_____

_____

78 Unit 6

Language in Action

7 Listen. Then answer the questions.

Mom: Jason, <u>come on</u>. It's time to get ready for school.

Jason: Oh, Mom. Do I have to?

Mom: Yes! Get your books ready while I <u>log on</u> to your virtual classroom.

Jason: OK. <u>Whoops!</u> I'm almost late for my English class!

Mom: At least you don't have to take the bus for an hour to school any more. Your teacher's right here for you all the time. You just need to <u>turn</u> him <u>on</u>!

Jason: Yes. But this robot teacher is stricter than the human ones were!

Mom: That's good. Maybe you'll learn more!

1 Where is Jason?

_____

2 Where does Jason go to school?

_____

3 How does Jason start classes with his teacher?

_____

4 Why does Jason prefer human teachers to robot teachers?

_____

8 Look at 7. Read the underlined expressions. How can you say them in other words? Match and write the letter.

_____ 1 come on   a I'm surprised.
_____ 2 log on   b Hurry! Let's go.
_____ 3 Whoops!   c start the computer
_____ 4 turn on   d switch on

9 Complete the dialog with the expressions in 8.

Mom: ¹_____, Emma. It's three o'clock. You'll be late for the soccer game.

Emma: Mom! The game was at two! I've missed it!

Mom: ²_____! Sorry, Emma. Never mind, it's raining anyway.

Emma: That's OK. I'll ³_____ to my laptop and play online.

Mom: Good idea. I'll ⁴_____ the lights for you. It's getting dark.

Unit 6 **79**

Language in Action

> Do you think we'll have cars 100 years from now?
>
> Yes, we will. But cars won't have drivers! They'll use computers.
>
> No, we won't. We'll have spaceships.

10 Look at the pictures. Complete the sentences. Use **will** or **won't**. Then listen and check your answers.

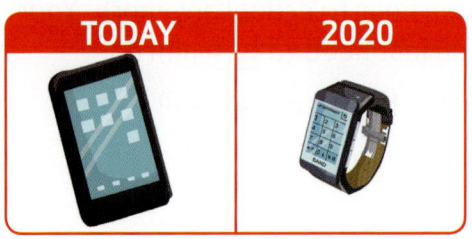

1 In 2020, smartphones _____ look the same as they do today.

2 In the future, you _____ wear your phone on your wrist.

3 In a few years from now, you _____ carry your computer in your pocket.

4 In the future, people _____ carry large tablets any more.

5 In the future, people probably _____ listen to music on an MP3 player.

6 With one Patchster patch near each ear, you and your friends _____ be able to listen to the same music at the same time.

11 Complete the questions and answers. Use **will** and **won't**.

1 Do you think computers _____ roll up like a piece of paper in the future?
_____

2 Do you think smartphones _____ be as smart as you?
_____

3 Do you think tablets _____ be bigger than they are today?
_____

4 Do you think robots _____ clean your room for you?
_____

80 Unit 6

Language in Action

Who **will use** video messaging in the future?	**Anyone** with a computer and internet access will use video messaging.
Who **will send** letters to communicate with friends in the future?	**No one/Nobody** will send letters to communicate with friends. **Everyone/Everybody** will use email. Well, **someone** might write a letter!

12 Read the class survey.

Mrs. Brown's Class Survey — Which activities will we do in 2020?

Will we . . .	Percentage of people who say "yes"
1 drive solar-powered cars?	100%
2 read paper books?	10%
3 go to Mars on a spaceship for a vacation?	0%
4 use non-digital cameras?	0%
5 send paper birthday cards?	20%

Mrs. Brown's class survey predicts that the following statements will come true. Circle the correct words.

1 _____ will drive solar-powered cars.
 a Everybody   b Someone

2 _____ will read paper books.
 a No one   b Someone

3 _____ will go to Mars on a spaceship for a vacation.
 a Someone   b Nobody

4 _____ will use non-digital cameras. We'll take pictures with digital cameras and smartphones.
 a No one   b Someone

5 _____ who likes to write will send paper birthday cards. Everyone else will send email cards.
 a Nobody   b Anyone

13 Circle the sentences in **12** that you agree with. Write one sentence that you don't agree with. Explain why.

I don't think that _____ because _____.

Unit 6 81

Content Connection | Science

14 Match the words to the definitions. Write the letters.

___ 1 assistive   a movements
___ 2 gestures   b medical
___ 3 surgical   c processes
___ 4 procedures   d always the same
___ 5 repetitive   e difficult
___ 6 complicated   f helpful

15 Listen and read. How will running robots help police?

Tomorrow's Robots

We all know that robots will be part of our future. In fact, there are already more than a million robots that work for us. Most of these robots do jobs that are too dirty, repetitive, or dangerous for people to do. In some factories, robots already make a lot of things, usually doing complicated tasks that people can't do. There are also robots today that are able to go to places that are too difficult or dangerous for humans to go to. Exploratory robots in space, for example, are able to explore parts of the universe in a way that humans cannot. Some robots can also explore deep underwater places that are too unsafe or too deep for people to reach. We aren't sure what the robotic creatures of the future will do, but many will surely be socially assistive robots, who will be able to move, talk, and make hand gestures. They will help people do things that they're unable to do. That's good, isn't it?

Firefighter Robots
One day, there will be robots that fight fires. Human firefighters will control the robots and guide them into burning buildings. One type of robot will look like a real firefighter. These robots will be able to walk, climb up ladders, and see through smoke. Another type will look like a snake, able to move through the air. These will help firefighters find people trapped in small places.

Running Robots
There might also be some robots that look like animals. They'll probably have four legs and be able to run very fast. They'll have bigger back legs than front legs so that they can jump, too. These robots will probably help police catch criminals. They'll catch the criminals because they'll be able to run faster than humans.

Jumping Robots
This robot won't look like an animal or person, but it'll do amazing things. It'll have wheels that move it from place to place. What's amazing about this robot is that it'll be able to jump very high. In fact, it might be able to jump over walls or onto rooftops. It'll help police see if there are dangerous things or people there.

16 Read **15** again and complete the chart.

Robot	What it will be able to do	Who and how it will help
1 Firefighter Robot		
2 Running Robot		
3 Jumping Robot		

17 Find and circle the words in **14**.

```
            q z i w
        a x c b w j t k
      r e p e t i t i v e
        s u r g i c a l w s
      a n s o e r o s d i a m
        i u m c s r m s i c y n
        l s f e t l p i t p z b
        q u p d u y l s i j n v
        a a e u r l i t o t e c
          l q r e q c i n y u s
            t e s t a v a s y
              s m v t e l
                    e
                    d
```

Which of the robots in 15 do you think will help people the most? Why?

THINK BIG

_____

_____

Unit 6 83

Grammar

18 Read and match.

1. In 30 years, will robots explore new planets?
2. In 2025, will we have robots as teachers?
3. In the future, will you go on vacation to the moon?
4. In 20 years, will people still put gas in their cars?

a. No, they won't. They'll have electric cars.
b. Yes, I will. There'll be hotels on the moon!
c. Yes, we will. There won't be human teachers.
d. No, they won't. Humans will explore new planets.

19 Complete the questions and answers with the words from the box.

| be | have | live | no | there (x2) | they | we | won't | will (x2) | yes |

1. **A:** In the future, _____ there be robots working in hospitals?
   B: No, there _____.
2. **A:** In 20 years, will people _____ robots to clean up their homes?
   B: No, _____ won't.
3. **A:** In 2030, will _____ still write letters?
   B: _____, we will.
4. **A:** In 50 years, will everyone _____ until they are 100 years old?
   B: _____, they won't.
5. **A:** Will _____ be only a few languages left in 2035?
   B: Yes, there _____.
6. **A:** Will there _____ enough food to feed the world in the future?
   B: No, _____ won't.

20 Unscramble and write questions. Then complete the answers.

1. will / a tablet / use / you / at school

   _____

   _____

   Yes, I _____.

2. he / will / an MP3 player / get / for his birthday

   _____

   _____

   No, he _____.

3. watch / they / will / on my laptop / a DVD

   _____

   _____

   Yes, _____.

4. a new smartphone / she / buy / will

   _____

   _____

   No, _____.

21 Rewrite the statements as questions.

1. In the future, there will be very cold winters and very hot summers.

   _____

2. Everyone will drive electric cars in 20 years.

   _____

3. People will buy only organic fruit and vegetables in 15 years.

   _____

4. You will use a computer all the time in your classroom in the future.

   _____

22 What do you think? Answer the questions in 21. Use Yes, … will or No, … won't.

1. _____
2. _____
3. _____
4. _____

Unit 6 85

Culture Connection | Around the World

23 Read and ✓.

1. to keep something from being harmed
   - a preserve ☐
   - b communicate ☐
2. when something no longer exists
   - a endangered ☐
   - b extinct ☐
3. a way of speaking a particular language
   - a dictionary ☐
   - b dialect ☐
4. a group of people about the same age
   - a generation ☐
   - b society ☐
5. to speak or write to someone
   - a communicate ☐
   - b pass on ☐
6. to speak a language easily and well
   - a official ☐
   - b fluently ☐

24 Read and complete with the words from the box. Then listen and check.

> alphabet   extinct   preserve   speakers   written

Saving Languages: Now and Long Ago

Did you know that at least one language becomes ¹_____ in the world every month? Languages are disappearing fast, and experts believe that in less than a hundred years, there will be only half of the languages left in the world that there are today. But there are some attempts to ²_____ endangered languages. For example, the Khang language and culture is one of the most endangered dialects in Vietnam. There are only 4,000 known speakers, and they don't have a ³_____ language. UNESCO (United Nations Educational, Scientific and Cultural Organization) decided to help keep the Khang language and culture from disappearing. UNESCO workers wrote down Khang traditions, developed a(n) ⁴_____, prepared materials for teaching the language in classes, and trained local ⁵_____ to teach those classes. Now, Khang speakers will be able to pass on the language to their children for generations to come. This seems like an effective way to preserve a language, doesn't it?

25 Read 24 again and circle T for true and F for false.

1 In a hundred years, there will be twice as many languages as there are today. T   F
2 The Khang language always had an alphabet. T   F
3 The Khang people are studying their language in classes today. T   F
4 Teaching the Khang language to young people will make the language endangered. T   F

26 Unscramble and write the words. Then match.

1 _____ aidctel
2 _____ eulftnyl
3 _____ repseerv
4 _____ ocmnumcitea
5 _____ ngeretnoia
6 _____ txenitc

a The next ☐ won't be able to understand the language.
b Languages, like plants and animals, can become ☐.
c He speaks a ☐ of an African language from the south.
d I can speak English, French, and Spanish ☐.
e It is important to ☐ languages that are disappearing.
f Can you ☐ in more than one language?

THINK BIG

How can people help save endangered languages?
_____
_____

Imagine you are the last speaker of a language. What do you want people to know about your language?
_____
_____

Unit 6 87

Writing | Diary entry

A diary is a special notebook. People often write about their day in this notebook. They write about the things that happened, and they often write about their feelings or thoughts during the day. Many people like writing in their diary every day. Some people share their diary entries. Some people write only for themselves. A diary entry is similar to a letter. It includes:

- a greeting (*Dear Diary, Hello*)
- an opening sentence. It usually describes the topic of your entry (*I'm very happy today.*)
- the body. It includes information about the topic.
- a closing (*Goodnight, Love, Bye*)
- your name

27 Label the parts of the diary entry.

1 _____ Dear Diary,

2 _____ We learned about the future in school today.

3 _____ I started thinking about my life in the future. In five years, everyone in my class will be in high school. I hope I'll have a boyfriend, and that he's nice! I won't be able to drive, but I hope that Mom and Dad will let me stay out late. I'm tired now, so I'll say goodbye.

4 _____ Goodnight,

5 _____ Pat

28 Look at 27. Circle the correct answers.

1 What comes after the greeting? **a** a period (.) **b** a comma (,) **c** nothing
2 What comes after the closing? **a** a period (.) **b** a comma (,) **c** nothing
3 What comes after the writer's name? **a** a period (.) **b** a comma (,) **c** nothing

29 Imagine your life six years from now. Write a diary entry about you and your life. Use 27 and 28 to help you.

Which one doesn't belong?

diary / blog / shopping list / letter

Review

30 Look at the chart. Then complete the sentences. Use **will** or **won't**.

My Predictions for the Year 2020	I don't think we'll have these things! Bye-bye!	I think these things will definitely be here!
1 text friends	with cell phones	with smartphones
2 write essays	on laptops – parents might use them	on tablets
3 listen to music	on MP3 players	with Patchster-like devices
4 buy items	mostly online using computers	mostly online using electronic gadgets

1 I think people _____ with cell phones. We _____ with smartphones.

2 We _____ on tablets in 2020. We _____ on laptops.

3 In the future, we _____ on MP3 players. We _____ with Patchster-like devices.

4 I think we _____ mostly online using our electronic gadgets. We _____ online using computers.

31 Look at 30. Complete the sentences. Use **Everybody** or **Nobody**.

1 _____ will use cell phones.
2 _____ will write essays on laptops.
3 _____ will use Patchster-like devices.
4 _____ will listen to music on MP3 players.

32 Answer the questions. Use your own ideas.

1 Will people carry umbrellas in the future? Why/Why not?

_____

2 Will we read only ebooks in the year 2025 instead of paper books? Why/Why not?

_____

Unit 6 **89**

Checkpoint | Units 4–6

1 Look at the pictures. What are they? Write the words.

SHOPPING AROUND

1 _____
2 _____
3 _____
4 _____

VACATION TIME

1 _____ 2 _____
3 _____ 4 _____

THE FUTURE

1 _____
2 _____
3 _____
4 _____

90 Checkpoint Units 4–6

2 Find or think of a song that talks about shopping, a vacation, or the future. Complete the chart.

Song title	
Singer	
Is the song in English? What language is the song in?	
What's it about?	
Why do you like listening to this song?	
Is it the most popular song now?	
What were you doing when you first heard it?	
Do you think it'll be popular next year?	

3 Write a review of the song for your school newspaper. Use the information in **1** and **2** to help you.

Checkpoint Units 4–6

UNIT 7 WHAT'S THAT?

1 Look at the pictures. Match the gadgets to their uses. Write the letters.

_____ **Picture 1** This is used for…

_____ **Picture 2** These are used for…

_____ **Picture 3** This is used for…

_____ **Picture 4** This is used for…

a listening to music. You wear this headband to listen to music comfortably, even while you sleep. It's a Music Headband.

b doing research. You ask it questions, and it tells you the answers. It helps you find information. It's Robo-pedia.

c watching movies. You put on these glasses and watch movies that only you can see. They're Movie Theater Glasses.

d drinking. You can fill it up with water and drink it. When you're finished, you can roll it up and put it away. It's a Roll-up Bottle.

2 Which gadgets in **1** do you like? Rate them. 1 = It's amazing! 2 = It's cool. 3 = It's OK. 4 = It's boring/not interesting.

a Robo-pedia _____   b Roll-up Bottle _____

c Movie Theater Glasses _____   d Music Headband _____

3 Match the old things to the modern things. Write the numbers.

1   2   3   4

a   b   c   d

___   ___   ___   ___

4 Write the names. Use the words from the box. Listen and circle the correct answers.

> cell phone   handheld game device   instant camera   transistor radio

1 A _____ is used to
   a play video games at home.   b play games outside.
2 A _____ is used mostly to
   a talk to people.   b record messages.
3 An _____ is used mostly to
   a take pictures.   b make movies.
4 A _____ is used to
   a record music and the news.   b listen to music and the news.

What do you think about the future of these items? Will we still use them in the future? Why/Why not?

> maps   telephone directories   watches

_____
_____

Unit 7

Reading | Skit

 5 Listen and read. Then answer the questions.

CAST
Ann, Jim (classmates) | **Miss Albany (teacher)**

SETTING: A Grade 6 classroom in the year 2015.
[The class finds a time capsule that the school made in 1990. They open it and are looking at the things inside it.]

Ann: *[picking up a thin square object]* Look at this. What is it?
Jim: *[takes it from her and looks at it carefully]* I'm not sure. It's plastic, and it has a metal rectangle on it.
Ann: Hmm… I think it was used for watching movies on a computer.
Jim: I don't think so. I don't think people could watch movies on computers in 1990.
Ann: You're right.
Jim: *[picking up a thick rectangular object]* And what's this? It's some kind of small machine.
Ann: *[presses one of the buttons and it starts working]* Hey, it's an old music player. *[Ann puts the headphones to her ears]*
Jim: *[putting his hands over his ears]* Oh, no! I don't want to listen to old music!
Ann: *[laughing]* Someone's going to say the same thing about our music in the future. I kind of like this music. I'm going to take it to my grandpa. He might remember this kind of music.

[A teacher enters]

Jim: *[holding up the thin square object]* Hello, Miss Albany. What's this?
Miss Albany: Oh, that's a floppy disk. People used them to keep information on from a computer. That way they had the information even if their computer didn't work.
Jim: I see.
Ann: It's fun looking at these old things.

1 What did Ann pick up?
_____

2 What did she think it was used for?
_____

3 Did Jim like the music?
_____

4 What did people use the square object for?
_____

6 Answer the questions.

How old does something have to be for you to think it is "old"? Why?
_____

Language in Action

7 Listen and read. Circle **T** for true and **F** for false.

Iris: What's in the box?

Laura: It's not a box. <u>See?</u> It doesn't open. My grandpa brought it back from China when he went there many years ago.

Iris: <u>Let's see.</u> It's hard and looks like it would break if you dropped it.

Laura: Well, it would! It's ceramic, like the plates and dishes we use for eating.

Iris: OK. But what is it? What's it used for?

Laura: <u>You won't believe it</u>, but it's a pillow!

Iris: A pillow? But it's so hard!

Laura: A long time ago, women in Asia had very beautiful hairstyles that took a lot of work to create. They didn't want to ruin them by sleeping on a soft pillow. So they just rested their necks on a ceramic pillow like this one. It was used for <u>keeping their hair in place</u>.

Iris: Gosh! That doesn't sound very comfortable.

1 The object is a pillow made of plastic.   T   F
2 It was used when women were sleeping.   T   F
3 Iris thinks it's a good pillow.   T   F

8 Look at **7**. Read the underlined expressions. How can you say them in other words? Match and write the letters.

_____ 1 See?
_____ 2 You won't believe it.
_____ 3 Let's see.
_____ 4 keep (their hair) in place

a It's surprising.
b Look closely.
c keep (their hair) from getting messy
d Let me think.

9 Complete the dialog. Use the expressions in **8**.

A: What were those bones used for?

B: ¹_____. Now I remember.
²_____, but those bones were used for a children's game called *knucklebones*!

A: How did women in ancient Greece ³_____ their clothes _____?

B: Well, look at this picture. ⁴_____? They wrapped a piece of cloth around themselves and used pins or belts.

Language in Action

What's it used for? | It's **used for** listening to music.
It's **used to** listen to music.

10 Match and write the letters.

____ 1 A hands-free ear piece is used for
____ 2 A cell phone is used to
____ 3 A video game system is used to
____ 4 A handheld game device is used for

a play video games.
b making phone calls.
c playing video games.
d make phone calls.

11 Look and read. Answer the questions with **used for** or **used to** and the words from the box.

finding where a place is   listen to music   make cars go   writing essays

1
A: What are they used for?
B: _____

2
A: What are they used for?
B: _____

3
A: What's it used for?
B: _____

4
A: What's it used for?
B: _____

Language in Action

What is it?	I'm not sure. It **may** be a small plate.
	It **might** be a salt dish.

12 What do you think these old things are? Use the words from the box and **may** or **might** to write sentences.

> abacus   egg beater   gramophone   washboard

1 _____

2 _____

3 _____

4 _____

13 Look at the items in **12**. What do you think they were used for? Write sentences with **used to**.

1 _____
2 _____
3 _____
4 _____

Unit 7 **97**

Content Connection | Social Science

14 Complete the chart with inventions. Use the words from the box.

> candle   cash register   combustion engine   plumbing

How the inventions help people	Invention
1 We can easily take a shower and wash dishes and clothes.	
2 We can travel by vehicles on land, water, and air.	
3 We can see at night when the lights go out.	
4 Stores can keep their money safe.	

15 Listen and read. Who invented the bendable straw?

Everyday Inventions

1 What do you think of when you hear the word *invention*? Do you think of electrical appliances, of which we find many in our homes and in our classrooms? Or do you think of cars, trains, and airplanes, which make it possible for us to travel to different places? There are so many useful inventions in the world today, without which our lives would be very different.

2 What do you know about the people who made these inventions? Who do you think of when you hear the word *inventor*? Do you think of Thomas Edison, the inventor of the light bulb, or Karl Benz, the inventor of the gasoline-powered car?

bendable straw

3 Not all inventors are world famous. In fact, we don't know the names of a lot of inventors who invented some of the small, useful things we use every day. For example, everyone knows about the bendable straw. But does anyone know the name Joseph Friedman? In 1937, he invented the bendable straw.

4 Joseph's brother owned a café. One day, Joseph was watching his youngest daughter drink a milkshake with a long straw. The straw was long, and she couldn't reach the end of it easily with her mouth. You may not see this as a problem, but Joseph did! He said, "Let's see. I'll put a metal screw into the straw, and wrap some wire around it on the outside of the straw." He tried it, and then he took the screw out. The straw could bend, and the bendable straw was born.

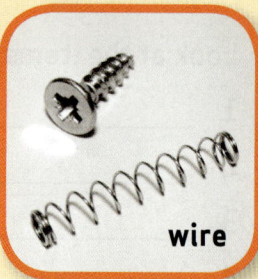
metal screw

wire

16 Read **15** again and answer the questions.

1 What did Thomas Edison invent?
   _____

2 Who invented the gasoline-powered car?
   _____

3 Who was with Joseph Friedman at his brother's café?
   _____

4 What problem was she having?
   _____

5 What did Joseph put inside and outside the straw?
   _____

6 What was the result?
   _____

17 Complete the sentences with the words from the box.

> bendable straw   invention   inventor   metal screw   wire

1 Did you know that the _____ of the dishwasher was a lady named Josephine Cochrane?

2 Many people find it easier to drink from a cola can with a _____.

3 You can buy handmade toys, decorations, and other crafts made from _____ at the African market.

4 Plumbing is an _____ that has brought running water to millions of people across the world.

5 You need to fix the chair leg with a _____ so that it does not fall off again.

THINK BIG

Imagine you're an inventor. What useful gadget would you invent? Describe how it could be used.

_____
_____
_____

Unit 7 99

Grammar

18 Read and match.

1 If you go to the history museum,
2 When I visit my grandfather,
3 You don't find old-fashioned TVs,
4 You learn how computers used to store information

a if you go to an electronics store.
b when you go to the Technology Center.
c you see old things like this gramophone.
d I like to play with his old radio.

19 Read and ✓.

1 If you're on vacation in New York,
 a you need American dollars.
 b you needed American dollars.

2 When we visit my cousins,
 a we took them gifts.
 b we take them gifts.

3 You can catch a cold
 a if you didn't wear a warm jacket.
 b if you don't wear a warm jacket.

4 I give my mother a big hug
 a when she picks me up from school.
 b when she picked me up from school.

5 When plants don't get enough water,
 a they die.
 b they died.

20 Complete the sentences with the correct form of the verbs in parentheses.

1 If Mom _____ (go) to the kitchen store, she always buys something.
2 When I do my homework, I _____ (not listen) to music or watch TV.
3 If she _____ (not finish) her dinner, she doesn't have ice cream.
4 When it _____ (be) fall, the leaves fall off the trees.
5 We swim if the sun _____ (shine).
6 They eat dinner when their father _____ (come) home.

21 Put the words in the correct order.

1 when / to London, / I go / the Buckingham Palace / I like to see
_____

2 lost / when / they don't get / a compass, / explorers use
_____

3 my bedroom / clean / I / when / from school / I get home
_____

4 and rests / drinks water / she / sick / she feels / if
_____

22 Complete the sentences for you. Use *if* or *when*.

1 _____, I watch a DVD at home.
2 _____, we eat breakfast late.
3 I play with my friends _____.
4 We don't do homework _____.

Culture Connection | Around the World

23 Match the words to the definitions. Write the letters.

____ 1 transform a a company that supplies goods for stores or businesses
____ 2 connect b something from nature which can be used, e.g. wood
____ 3 supplier c to change
____ 4 combine d to join one thing to another
____ 5 natural resource e to mix together

24 Listen and read. Match the headings A–C to the paragraphs 1–3.

A Kingfisher-Inspired Train
B An Animal that Inspires you
C Elephant-Inspired Arm and Hand

Animals Inspire Inventions

Animals move in ways that are unique. People can't swim like dolphins or turn their heads around like owls. Scientists are using computer technology to study the movement of animals. Then they use this knowledge to create interesting inventions that help people.

1 Engineers in Germany studied the elephant's trunk. They wanted to create a robotic arm and hand that could move just like an arm and could work safely with humans in factories, transforming the way certain products are made. They created a bionic handling assistant. The assistant looks like an elephant's trunk with a claw, and it's very light and very safe. When it accidentally hits a human, it moves back. It's also very gentle. It can pick up an egg!

2 Japan is one of the world's leading suppliers of new technology. A Japanese engineer, Ejii Nakatsu, wanted to solve a problem. The fastest trains in Japan, the bullet trains, made a very loud noise when they came out of tunnels. Trains also slowed down when they came out of tunnels. Ejii loved birds, and he knew that kingfishers dive into the water from the air with no splash. This is because of the shape of their beaks. He worked to change the front of the trains to be more like a kingfisher beak. The problem was solved.

3 These are just two inventions inspired by animals. So the next time you see an animal, look at it closely. Watch how it moves and notice which part of its body it uses. There might be an invention inspired by it! Think of a giraffe's long neck, a chameleon's sticky tongue, or a crocodile's powerful jaws. Or what about a butterfly's wings, a monkey's tail, or a penguin's flippers? Can you think of how any of these can be combined with technology to inspire a new invention?

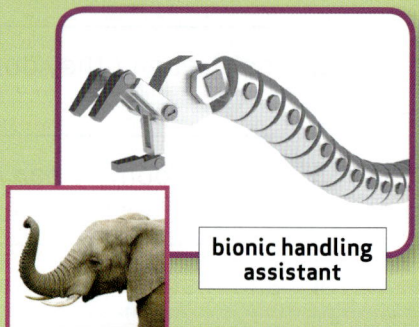
bionic handling assistant

bullet train

kingfisher

25 Read **24** again and answer the questions.

1 What do scientists study to create helpful inventions?
   _____

2 What inspired the bionic handling assistant?
   _____

3 Where is the bionic handling assistant used?
   _____

4 What two problems did bullet trains have?
   _____

5 How were these problems solved?
   _____

26 Complete the sentences with the words from **23**.

1 My father's business is the main _____ of organic fruit to a large supermarket in our town.
2 Water is a very important _____, which we all have to save and use carefully.
3 When baking a cake, you have to _____ the ingredients together in a mixing bowl.
4 It's amazing to see a caterpillar _____ into a butterfly in just a few weeks.
5 The new railway line will _____ different places around the city.

THINK BIG

Complete the chart with the inventions. Then make up one of your own.

Climbing rope   Fast swimming suit   Moving ladder

Animal movement	Invention
Monkey's tail	
Shark skin	
Giraffe's neck	

Unit 7 **103**

Writing | Description: Object

> When you write a description of an object, it's good to write about:
> - the way it looks (**It's** red, large, and round. **It looks like** an elephant's trunk.)
> - the things it has and can do (**It has** two legs. **It can** go very fast.)
> - what it's used for (**It's used to** carry heavy things.)
>
> Include as much information as you can so the readers can see a picture of that object in their mind.

27 Read this paragraph about an amazing object. What is it?

> This object is really amazing. It's rectangular. It's white or black with a large screen on one side. It looks like a thin book, but you can't open or close it. You can carry it everywhere in your bag. You can read and listen to music on it. It has a camera, so you can take pictures and even videos with it. You can also send and receive emails on it. It's used to entertain people on long trips. It's a _____.

28 Underline the sentences in 27 that describe the way the object looks. Circle the sentences that describe the things it has/can do. Underline twice the things it is used for.

29 Think of an invention. Complete the idea web.

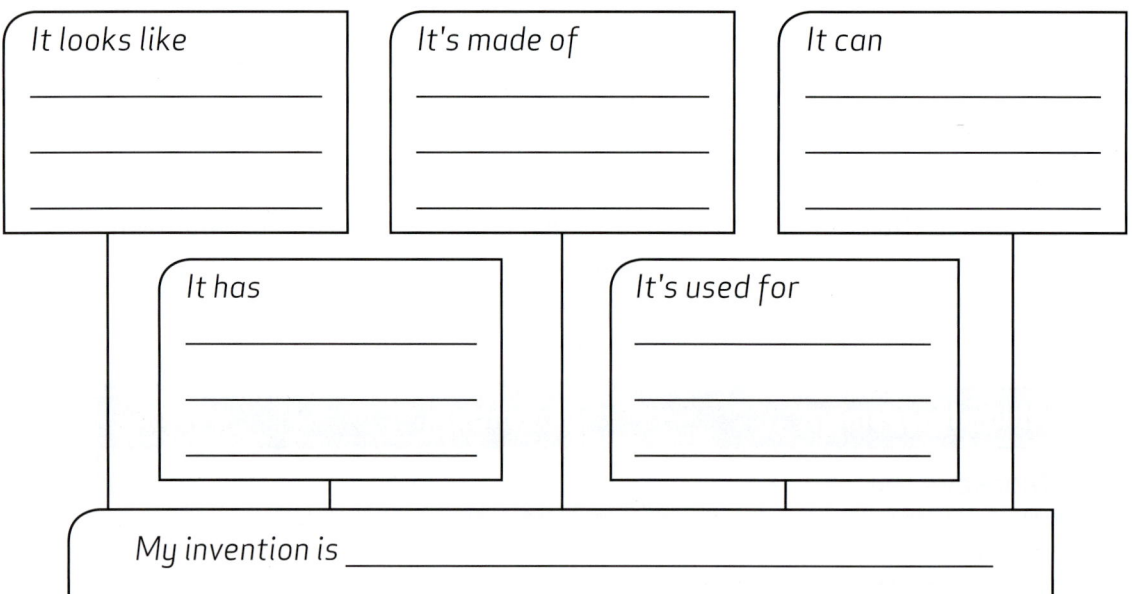

30 Write a description of an invention in your notebook. Use 27, 28, and 29 to help you.

104 Unit 7

Review

31 Look at the code. Write the words. Then match the words and pictures. Write the numbers.

●	▲	■	▬	◆	◈	▲	▼	▶	◀	=	+	÷
a	b	c	d	e	f	g	h	i	j	k	l	m

✗	O	◇	□	▭	✱	!	]	?	#	%	▼	◣
n	o	p	q	r	s	t	u	v	w	x	y	z

1 ▼ ● ✗ ▬ ✱ - ◈ □ ◆ ◆   ◆ ● □   ◇ ▶ ◆ ■ ◆

2 ▶ ✗ ✱ ! ● ✗ !   ■ ● ÷ ◆ □ ●    a ___

3 ! □ ● ✗ ✱ ▶ ✱ ! O □   □ ● ■ ▶   b ___

 c ___

32 Imagine it's the year 2023. How will you talk about these things? Write the questions. Complete the answers. Use **used to** and **used for** and the words from the box.

> finding where a place is   listen to music   making cars go   play fun games

1 **A:** These are _____.
   B: _____?
   A: They'_____.

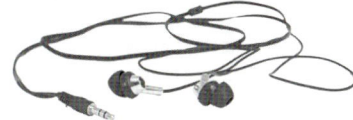

2 **A:** This is a _____.
   B: _____?
   A: They're _____.

3 **A:** This is a _____.
   B: _____?
   A: It's _____.

4 **A:** This is a _____.
   B: _____?
   A: It's _____.

unit 8
WHERE DO THEY COME FROM?

1 Look at the pictures. Read the name of the inventions that come from these places. Do any surprise you?

Italy: eyeglasses, radio, piano

India: chess, ink, pajamas

England: jigsaw puzzle, matches, combustion engine

China: sunglasses, noodles, paper lantern

2 Circle the inventions that you use or see every day.

jigsaw puzzle	chess	matches	eyeglasses
combustion engine	ink	pajamas	piano
noodles	radio	chess	paper lantern

3 Look at 1 and 2. Where do most of the items that you circled come from?

Most of the products that I use or see were invented in _____.

4 What items that you use every day were invented in your country?

_____

106 Unit 8

5 Read. Circle the two correct answers.

1 These are made mostly of metal.
 a silver earrings   b a plane   c a basketball

2 These are made of rubber.
 a kitchen gloves   b T-shirts   c rain boots

3 Some of these are made of wool.
 a candles   b blankets   c sweaters

4 Some of these are made of cotton.
 a T-shirts   b jackets   c tires

5 These are made of clay.
 a cups   b blankets   c plates

6 Listen. What are the things? Number them in the order you hear them. Then write the names.

| balls | clothes | teacup | train |

Clothes are made of a lot of different materials. Which materials can keep us warm? Which material can keep us dry?

_____

Unit 8 **107**

Reading | Travel forum

7 Listen and read. Then answer the questions.

beach_boy: My family is planning a vacation this year. I want to go somewhere warm and sunny. I'd love to spend a lot of time on a beautiful sandy beach. Hiking would be fun, too. Where should we go?

travel_tracy: Go to the island of Korčula, one of the islands in Croatia. Fun things to do and see can be found everywhere, and it's easy to visit other islands, too. Korčula is known for its beautiful beaches and wonderful summer weather, but there are also places to go hiking and biking. Take time to walk around the historic fortified town of Korčula and photograph the amazing scenery. Go on a boat trip to the neighboring islands and enjoy eating fresh seafood, too. You'll definitely enjoy a vacation on this great island!

1 Where is Korčula?

_____

2 What's Korčula known for?

_____

3 What's special about the town?

_____

4 What two things would you like to do on Korčula? Why?

_____

_____

_____

Language in Action

8 Listen and read. Then circle **T** for true and **F** for false.

Suzy: Maybe I can find something for my sister here. It's her birthday next week.

Rosa: I definitely think you can. That table over there has stacks of handmade cotton blouses. They're made in Hungary.

Suzy: They're beautiful.

Rosa: Look, Margaret's wearing one. See how it's worn? The strings are pulled and tied in the front. It's a nice look.

Suzy: My sister would love it! But look, the one that I like is torn.

Rosa: I'm sure it can be fixed. Look, the sign says, "These are all second-hand clothes." Let's ask Margaret's mom if it can be repaired.

Suzy: Great idea!

1 It's Suzy's mom's birthday soon.   T   F
2 Rosa likes the blouses.   T   F
3 Suzy thinks her sister will like the blouse.   T   F
4 The blouse Suzy likes is new.   T   F

9 Look at **8**. Read the underlined expressions. Match the expressions to their meaning. Write the letters.

____ 1 stacks of
____ 2 handmade
____ 3 second-hand

a not new – having been worn in the past by someone else
b a lot of
c made by using your hands and not by machines in a factory

10 Complete the dialog with the expressions in **9**.

A: Look at these amazing scarves. Why are they so cheap?

B: I imagine it's because they're ¹_____. But they look new.

A: I'm going to buy the red and yellow one.

B: I love this local craft fair. ²_____ these things look ³_____!

A: I know. I love things that are made by hand.

Language in Action

> That watch **is made** in Switzerland.
> Those bananas **are grown** in Ecuador.
>
> The first pizza **was** probably **made** in Italy.
> The first noodles **were** probably **made** in China.

11 Match the three forms of the verbs. Draw lines.

	Simple Present	Simple Past	Past Participle
1	eat	flew	flown
2	fly	made	invented
3	grow	ate	raised
4	introduce	invented	grown
5	invent	mined	eaten
6	produce	introduced	made
7	make	produced	introduced
8	mine	raised	mined
9	raise	grew	produced

12 Complete the sentences. Use the simple present passive form of the verb in parentheses.

1 Olives _____. (grow in Greece)

2 Sheep _____. (raise in New Zealand)

3 Many cars _____. (make in China)

4 Gold _____. (mine in South Africa)

5 Denim _____. (produce in many countries)

Language in Action

13 Look. Complete the sentences. Use the simple past passive form of the verb in parentheses.

1 Chess _____ probably _____ in India. (invent)
2 In 1783, the first hot air balloon _____. (fly)
3 The first shopping cart _____ in 1937. (make)
4 The gramophone, or record player, _____ in 1877 by Thomas Edison. (introduce)

14 Unscramble the words. Use the words to write sentences. Use the simple present passive form of the verb.

1 anabsan   wrog
_____ _____
_____ in Ecuador.

2 lhsels   ndfi
_____ _____
_____ on the beach.

3 roscec   lypa
_____ _____
_____ all over the world.

4 tobos   emka
_____ _____
_____ of rubber.

Content Connection | Science

15 Read and match. Write the letters.

___ 1 fresh produce a something that has a harmful effect on air, land, or water
___ 2 pollution b foodstuffs that go bad quickly
___ 3 imported c usual or normal
___ 4 country of origin d brought from a different country
___ 5 typical e where something or someone comes from

16 Read and complete with the words from the box. Then listen and check.

> distribution center   fresh   local   pollution   typical

Farmers' Markets and Our Future

Where does your family buy fresh fruit and vegetables from? Do you go to a supermarket or do you go to a farmers' market? All over the world, farmers gather on specific days in specific places, like a park or parking lot, to sell their produce directly to customers. Their produce is fresh – often picked just the day before! It's also seasonal, which means that in the summer you can buy only summer fruits and vegetables, and in the winter you can buy only winter fruits and vegetables. Some farmers' markets also have live entertainment like singers and musicians and sell things other than produce, like crafts made by ¹_____ people. So they can be a great place to find and buy gifts for people and just to have fun!

Shopping at a farmers' market can be a good thing to do. Here's why:

A   You can meet local farmers and learn about their produce. You can find out what's in season, and some farmers may give advice on how to prepare and cook their produce.

B   Locally-grown food is very ²_____. It hasn't been stored or refrigerated for long, and it hasn't been transported far. So every bite tastes good!

C   The food doesn't have to travel a long distance from the farm to a ³_____ and then to you. It goes only a short distance from the farm to you. This results in less ⁴_____ and helps keep the environment clean.

D   Buying from local farmers can help the environment in other ways, too. When farmers don't make enough money to live on, they are often obliged to sell their farms to land developers. The developers build houses and buildings on the farmland. More houses may cause more pollution and greater demands on natural resources like rivers, lakes, and forests in the area.

E   A ⁵_____ farm is a beautiful place. It has fields, meadows, woods, and ponds. It provides homes for animals like rabbits, birds, and deer. So if the farm disappears, the animals may have nowhere to live, and you may have nowhere to go to enjoy nature's beauty.

Next time your mom buys vegetables, think about asking her to go to a local farmers' market. You'll have a fun time, and you'll support your local community.

17 Read 16 again and circle the correct answers.

1 Farmers' markets are always ____.
   a in different places
   b in the same place

2 Buying locally helps the environment because ____.
   a farmers sell the produce cheaply
   b produce travels a short distance from the farm to the market

3 If farmers don't have enough money to live on, they sometimes ____.
   a sell their farms
   b build houses

4 If farmers sell their farms, ____.
   a animals will be able to stay on the land
   b some animals will lose their home

18 Complete the sentences with the words from the box.

> customers   developers   environment   produce   seasonal

1 A farmers' market is a great place to buy fresh _____, some of which has been picked that morning.

2 At a farmers' market, the _____ are people who choose to buy locally-grown foods rather than imported foods from a supermarket.

3 You can always buy _____ fruit and vegetables at a farmers' market, but it is difficult to find anything that is out of season.

4 Pollution of the _____ damages our natural resources.

5 Some _____ bought the farm and built several new houses there.

THINK BIG

It's summer. What seasonal fruit could you buy at a local farmers' market in your country? Make a list.

_____

_____

Grammar

19 Read and circle.

1 She's the girl **who** / **which** loves singing.
2 Winter is a time **that** / **when** the days are short and the nights are long.
3 They are the children **who** / **whose** grandparents live in Italy.
4 Here's a shopping cart **that** / **where** we can use.
5 He goes on vacation to places **which** / **where** he can swim in the ocean.
6 I love chocolate **when** / **which** has nuts in it.

20 Complete the sentences with the words from the box.

> that   when   where   which   whose   who

1 Why don't you wear the wool hat _____ your grandma knitted for you?
2 He's the man _____ pants are too short.
3 Here are some shells _____ we found on the beach.
4 I'm the one _____ is interested in farming.
5 The farmers' market is the place _____ you can buy delicious strawberries.
6 Early morning is the time _____ you should water the plants.

21 Link the sentences using the word in parentheses.

1 That's the farm. My uncle works there. (where)
_____

2 I love eating peaches. They are juicy. (that)
_____

3 Have you seen my shoes? I wore them yesterday. (which)
_____

4 She made a card for her friend. Her friend's pet cat is lost. (whose)
_____

114 Unit 8

22 Read and match. Then rewrite as one sentence using who, when, or which.

1 The T-shirts are drying.
2 The girl is walking in the rain.
3 Would you like some tea?
4 Lunchtime is the time.

a The tea is made.
b I sit with my friends and talk.
c Mehmet hung the T-shirts on the line.
d The girl loves her new boots.

1 _____
2 _____
3 _____
4 _____

23 Complete the sentences for you. Use who, which, that, whose, when, or where.

1 I really like my teacher
_____.

2 My favorite story is one
_____.

3 Evenings are the time
_____.

4 I know a person
_____.

5 My home is a place
_____.

Culture Connection | Around the World

24 Complete the sentences with the words from the box.

> chemical   engineer   novelty   poisonous   refrigerator

1 When the scientist added one _____ to another, he caused an explosion.
2 You always have to wash your hands if you touch something _____.
3 A _____ is the best way to keep food cold and fresh.
4 Eating sushi is a _____ for me.
5 My grandfather was a(n) _____ who built several bridges in Australia.

25 Listen and read. Why do people invent things?

Problems and Inventions

1 All over the world, there are objects that people use and things people do, which have been invented. Why do people invent things? Where do ideas for inventions come from? There's a saying that, "Necessity is the mother of invention." This means that people invent things because there's a problem, and they want to solve the problem. Let's read about two very different things that were invented to solve two very different problems…

2 In 1912, American engineer Otto Frederick Rohwedder had an idea. He wanted to invent a machine that could slice a whole loaf of bread. He built his first bread slicer in 1917, but it was destroyed in a fire. In 1927, he had enough money to build another one. But he realized he had a problem – the bread became stale after it was cut. He then had another idea, and he built a bread slicer that sliced the bread and then wrapped it so that it wouldn't get stale so quickly. So the next time you see a loaf of sliced bread, think about Otto Frederick Rohwedder's invention and how useful it is to us every day!

3 Have you ever heard of a game called Hacky Sack? It's also known as Footbag. The Hacky Sack or the Footbag is a novelty item that was invented by John Stalberger and Mike Marshall. In 1972, Mike Marshall made a small beanbag and kicked it in the air with his foot for fun. That same year John Stalberger had knee surgery. His knee exercises after surgery were boring, so he looked for a more fun way to exercise. He and Mike shared ideas, and the game of Hacky Sack was born. Now, there's a great way to put an old beanbag to good use… Why don't you organize a game of Hacky Sack or Footbag with your friends in the park? You can even play it indoors on a rainy day!

4 Society needs inventors. Our lives are better because inventors are problem solvers. Many of them solve everyday problems by inventing something useful we can use or do. Think of a problem in your home or at your school. Can you invent something to solve it?

26 Read **25** again and answer the questions.

1 What did Otto Frederick Rohwedder invent?
_____

2 What problem did he have?
_____

3 How did he solve the problem?
_____

4 What problem did John Stalberger have?
_____

5 How did he and Mike Marshall solve this problem?
_____

27 Read and ✓.

1 Something you need to have or do
   a necessity ☐   b possibility ☐
2 To cut something quickly and easily
   a wrap ☐   b slice ☐
3 No longer fresh
   a whole ☐   b stale ☐
4 A medical procedure where a part of someone's body is cut open to repair it
   a surgery ☐   b invention ☐
5 All the people in a large area and the way they live
   a society ☐   b school ☐

THINK BIG

What's the biggest problem in your home? What could you invent to solve it?
_____
_____
_____

Writing | Persuasive writing

When you write a persuasive paragraph, you want your reader to agree with your opinion. A good persuasive paragraph gives a strong main opinion and reasons for that opinion. Your reasons make your opinion stronger and more believable.

Opinion: *The South of France is a perfect place for a vacation.*

Reasons: *It has beautiful beaches with wonderful swimming and nice scenery.*

There are wonderful street markets, and the local food is delicious.

There are interesting and historic towns to visit, too, such as Nice and Montpellier.

28 Read the persuasive paragraph. Then answer the questions.

¹Cape Town is famous all over the world because it's a wonderful vacation destination. It's located at the tip of Africa in South Africa. ²You won't be bored here because there are lots of fun things to do. ³You can swim and sunbathe at Camps Bay, a favorite beach, and you can surf here, too. ⁴You can go on bus tours around the city or boat tours to see dolphins, seals, and humpback whales. ⁵You can also hike up Table Mountain or go up in a cable car. The view from the top is amazing! ⁶Cape Town is full of wonderful adventures for everyone. Why not choose it for your next vacation?

1 Which sentence is the main opinion? _____
2 How many reasons are given for that opinion? _____
3 Which sentences are the reasons? _____
4 Do you want to go there? Why/Why not? _____

29 Think of a nice vacation spot.
Complete the chart with your ideas.

- Name the vacation spot
- Give your opinion
- Explain your reason
- Give a second reason
- Give a third reason

30 Use your chart in **29** to write a persuasive paragraph about your vacation spot.

THINK BIG

Think of two reasons why people should visit your country for a vacation.

Review

31 Circle the products that can be made of the materials in the chart.

Wool	Rubber	Cotton	Metal	Clay
rug	comb	plate	shopping cart	pottery
scarf	boots	towels	cola can	produce
cola can	paper	jeans	watch	bowls
blanket	tire	plane	food	flower pot

32 Read and circle the correct answers.

1 Coffee _____ in Costa Rica, and you can visit coffee farms there.
   a was grown   b is grown

2 Beautiful glass _____ in Italy. You can buy it in expensive stores.
   a was made   b is made

3 Chocolate nut bars _____ in Canada.
   a were created   b are created

4 Fantastic watches _____ in Switzerland, and stores all over the world sell them.
   a are made   b were made

33 Complete the sentences with the correct form of the verb in parentheses.

1 Jars _____ from glass. (make)
2 Apples _____ in Italy and are very popular in the fall. (grow)
3 Matches _____ in England in 1827. (invent)
4 The earliest noodles _____ in China a long, long time ago. (eat)

34 Read and circle the correct words.

1 Here's the jigsaw puzzle **that** / **who** my grandpa gave me.
2 That's the beach **when** / **where** I lost my shoe.
3 Late afternoon is **when** / **which** she often goes for a run.
4 Those are the children **who** / **whose** coats I'm holding.

HOW ADVENTUROUS ARE YOU?

1 Listen and match. Write the number.

2 Read about the food in the pictures in 1. Rate them 1 = I really want to try it! 2 = I might want to try it. 3 = I never want to try it! Write your ratings.

1. This Filipino dessert is called Buko Pandan. It looks pretty, and it has a wonderful sweet taste.

2. Tandoori chicken is a popular traditional dish from India. It is made with chicken and spices like pepper and curry. It tastes hot and spicy!

3. Chinese soup has tofu in it. It's hot and sour. It has a very unusual taste!

4. Marinated octopus is a traditional seafood dish from Greece. The octopus is left in olive oil, lemon juice, and herbs for a short time. It's delicious!

3 How adventurous with food are you? Look at your ratings and ✓ your answer.

☐ I'm very adventurous. I rated most of the food a **1**.
☐ I'm somewhat adventurous. I rated most of the food a **2**.
☐ I'm not adventurous at all. I rated most of the food a **3**.

4 Listen and ✓ the words you hear for each food.

		unusual	tasty	popular	raw	spicy	sweet	traditional	delicious
1	gazpacho								
2	sushi								
3	tagine								
4	spumoni								

5 What food do you like? What food don't you like? What does it taste like?

_____

_____

Name a traditional food from your country. Then circle words to describe it.

_____

hot / raw / sweet / spicy / cold / sour

unusual / popular / delicious

Unit 9 **121**

Reading | Interview

6 Listen and read. Then answer the questions.

LIFE ON a BOAT

Eleven-year-old Glenn Dodd has lived on a boat with his family for the past two years. A local radio station is interviewing him.

Interviewer: Today on *Awesome Adventures*, we're talking to 11-year-old Glenn Dodd. Glenn's family has lived on a boat and has traveled around Australia for the last two years. Tell me, Glenn, what's it like living on a boat?

Glenn Dodd: Well, in the beginning it was really hard. There are four people in my family and a dog. The boat is small, so we were always very close to each other.

Interviewer: Wow! I'm sure that was tough sometimes.

Glenn Dodd: Yes, we had to learn to get along, or my dad said he'd throw us into the ocean!

Interviewer: That would make me behave, too! What do you like the most about life on a boat?

Glenn Dodd: Well, probably all the new things I can try.

Interviewer: Like what? Give me an example.

Glenn Dodd: Well, I've eaten alligator meat a few times. And I've scuba dived with stingrays. That was a little scary!

Interviewer I can imagine it was! Now tell me, after two years, would you rather live on a boat or in a house?

Glenn Dodd: Honestly, I really want to live in a house now, like my friends. Actually, my family has decided to go back home next month. So, soon, I'm going to be a land creature again.

Interviewer: Well, good luck, Glenn. That's all the time we have. Thanks again for sharing your story.

1 Where does Glenn Dodd live now? _____
2 What does Glenn like most about living there? _____
3 Do you think Glenn is an adventurous person? Why/Why not? _____

Language in Action

7 Listen. Then circle the correct answers.

Allie: Hi, Roberto. Let's do something on Saturday afternoon.

Roberto: That sounds good, Allie. But I have a lesson on Saturday.

Allie: You have lessons on Saturdays?

Roberto: Yes. I'm learning Chinese!

Allie: Chinese? Really?

Roberto: Yes. It's really interesting. Have you ever studied another language?

Allie: Well, I can speak English and Spanish. But I've never studied another language.

Roberto: It's a lot of fun. And I'm learning a lot. I can say so many things in Chinese already.

Allie: That's amazing! How do you say *hello* in Chinese?

Roberto: Ni hao, Allie!

Allie: Hola, Roberto!

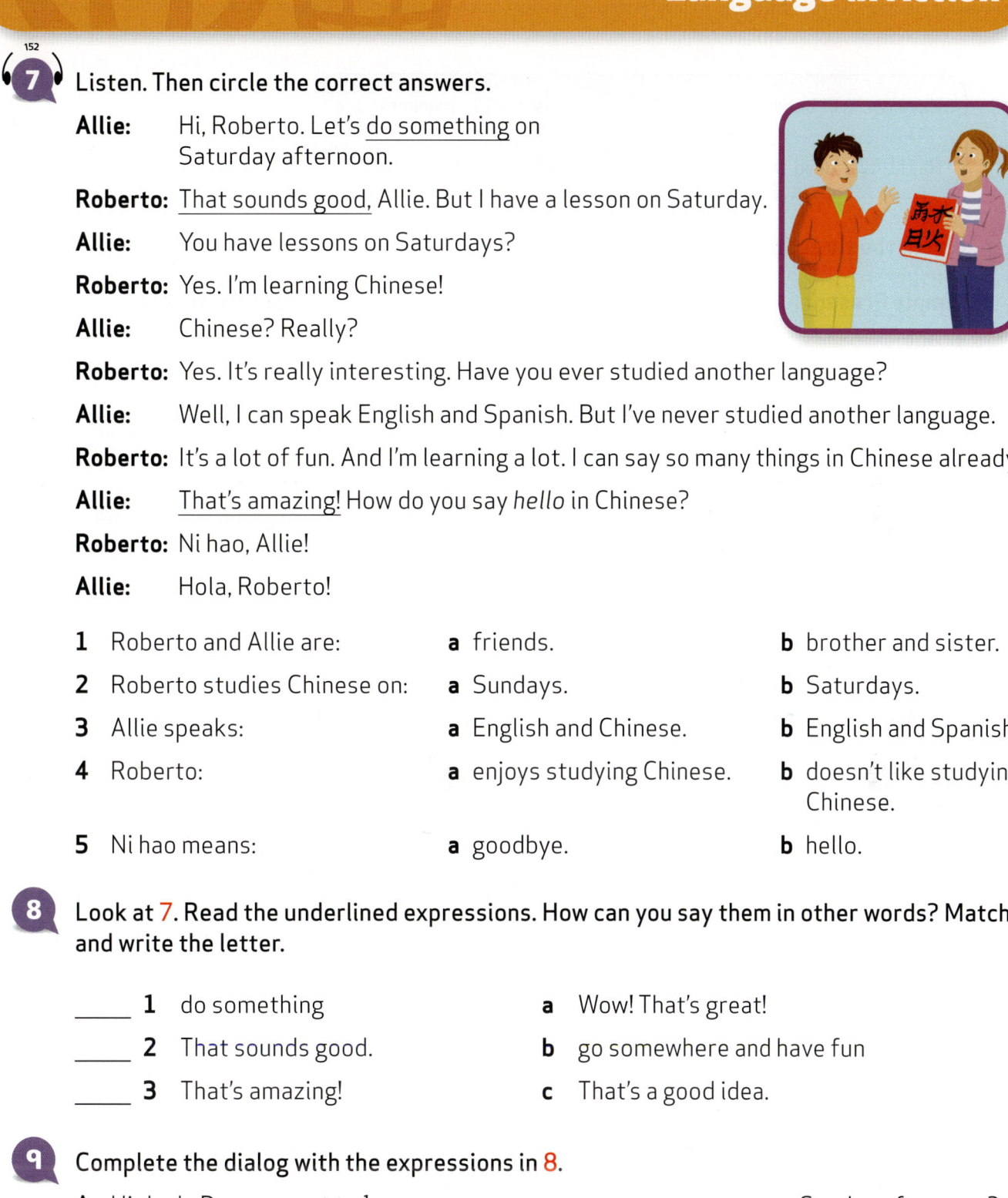

1	Roberto and Allie are:	a friends.	b brother and sister.
2	Roberto studies Chinese on:	a Sundays.	b Saturdays.
3	Allie speaks:	a English and Chinese.	b English and Spanish.
4	Roberto:	a enjoys studying Chinese.	b doesn't like studying Chinese.
5	Ni hao means:	a goodbye.	b hello.

8 Look at 7. Read the underlined expressions. How can you say them in other words? Match and write the letter.

_____ 1 do something   a Wow! That's great!

_____ 2 That sounds good.   b go somewhere and have fun

_____ 3 That's amazing!   c That's a good idea.

9 Complete the dialog with the expressions in 8.

A: Hi, Jack. Do you want to ¹_____ on Sunday afternoon?

B: ²_____. Do you want to go to the movies? I have two tickets, and they were free!

A: ³_____. Where did you get them from?

B: They were a present.

Unit 9 **123**

Language in Action

Have you ever been to a concert?	Yes, I have./No, I haven't.
Has he ever been skydiving?	Yes, he has./No, he hasn't.

10 Match the three forms of the verbs. Draw lines.

Simple Present	Simple Past	Past Participle
1 act	fell	gone
2 break	moved	fallen
3 fall	swam	won
4 go	broke	acted
5 have	acted	swum
6 move	won	broken
7 swim	went	had
8 win	had	moved

11 Unscramble the questions. Then look and write the answers.

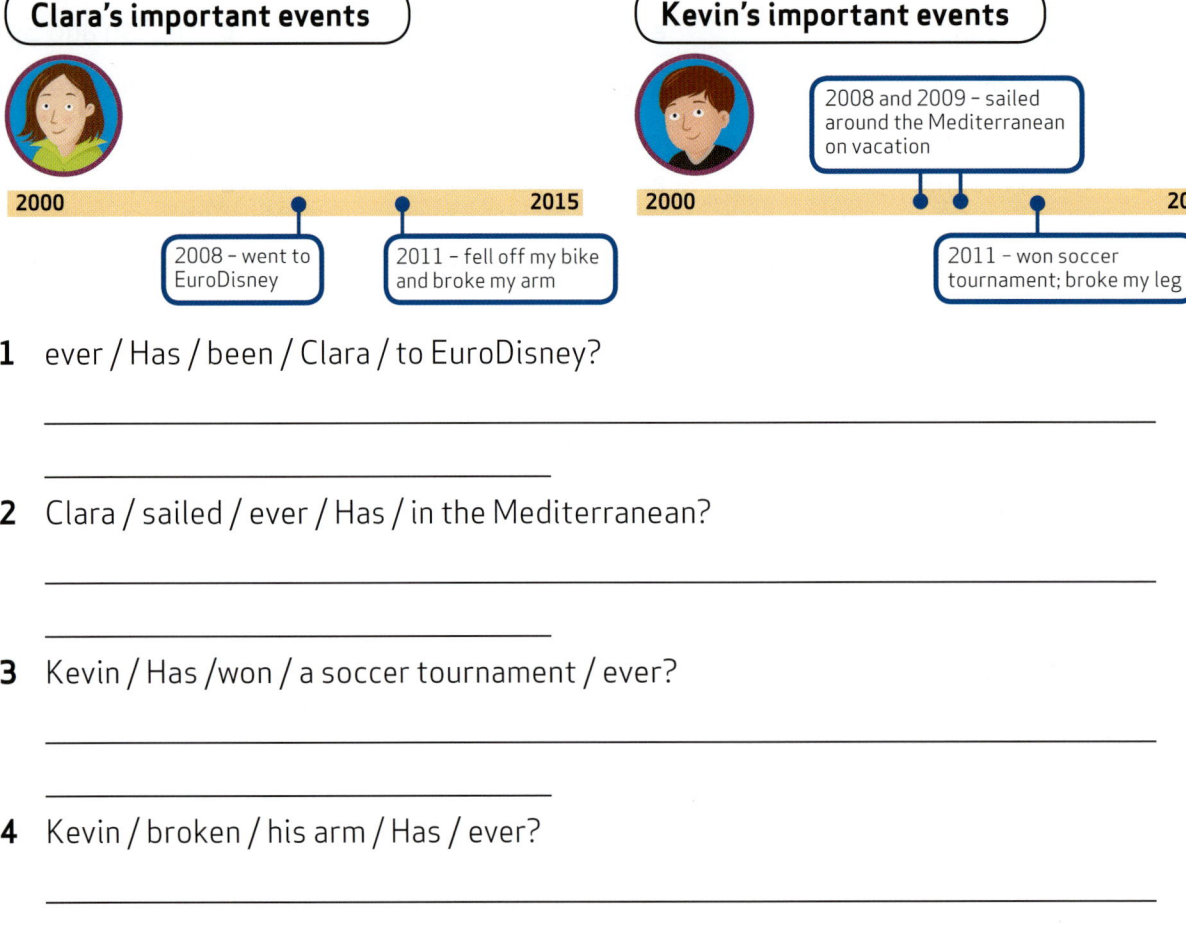

1 ever / Has / been / Clara / to EuroDisney?

_____

_____

2 Clara / sailed / ever / Has / in the Mediterranean?

_____

_____

3 Kevin / Has / won / a soccer tournament / ever?

_____

_____

4 Kevin / broken / his arm / Has / ever?

_____

_____

Language in Action

| Would they rather play soccer or watch it? | They'd rather play soccer. |

I'd = I would
you'd = you would
he'd = he would
she'd = she would
they'd = they would

12 Follow the lines. Make guesses and answer the questions.

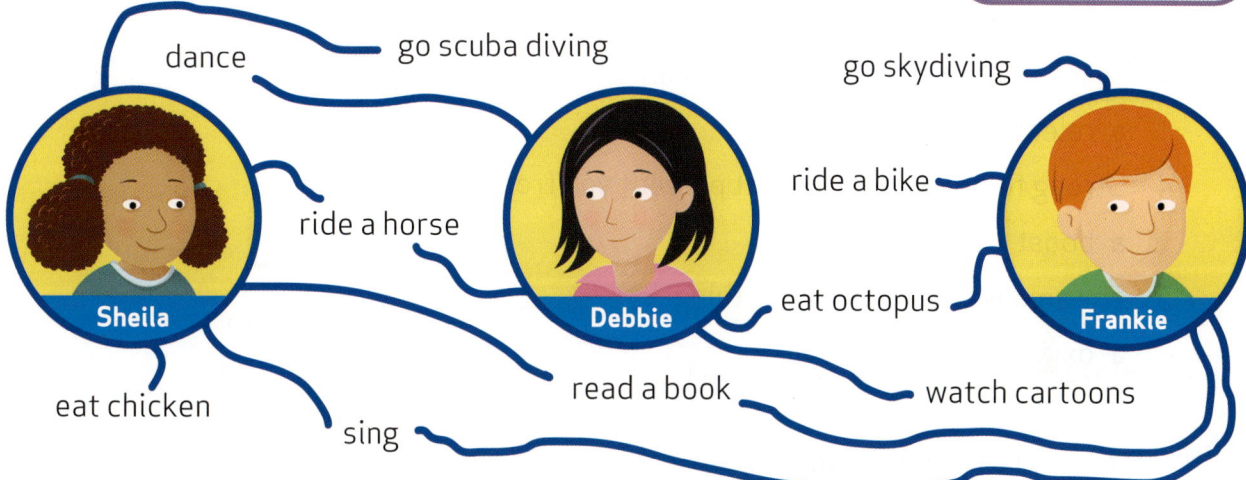

1 Would Sheila rather go skydiving or go scuba diving?
   _____

2 Would Sheila and Debbie rather ride a bike or ride a horse?
   _____

3 Would Frank rather eat chicken or eat octopus?
   _____

4 Would Frank and Sheila rather watch cartoons or read a book?
   _____

13 Answer the questions for you.

1 Would you rather eat chicken or eat octopus?
   _____

2 Would you rather ride a bike or ride a horse?
   _____

3 Would you rather go skydiving or go scuba diving?
   _____

Content Connection | Science

14 Read and ✓.

1 A chemical that your body produces when you are excited, frightened, or angry.
   a adrenal glands ☐   b adrenalin ☐

2 A chemical which your body produces that affects your body.
   a hormone ☐   b oxygen ☐

3 To let go of something (or someone).
   a release ☐   b protect ☐

4 Strong feelings of worry that prevent you from relaxing.
   a boost ☐   b stress ☐

5 The smallest part of a living thing.
   a oxygen ☐   b cell ☐

15 Listen and read. Why do some people race motorcycles at very high speeds?

Extreme Sports

Many people exercise to relax and to release stress. Sports like walking, swimming, and yoga are good ways to relax. But other people like sports that are exciting and may even be dangerous, like motorcar racing, skiing, and rock climbing. These people love the feel of adrenalin rushing through their bodies, giving them that extra boost of energy. Adrenalin is a hormone that our adrenal glands produce when we're excited, afraid, or angry. The information it gives our cells causes our heart to beat faster. This means more oxygen in our blood. The sudden boost of this hormone is called an adrenalin rush. Let's read about two extreme sports that give people an adrenalin rush.

Freeriding
Freeriding is like big wave surfing on snow. Skiers go to the top of a very high, steep mountain and ski down it. There are no paths for them to follow – they just follow the natural paths down the mountain. Where does the adrenalin rush come from? They go down the mountain very, very fast because the slopes that they ski down are very steep. Some slopes are almost at ninety degrees to the ground. They also fly in the air in some places, over rock-covered snow cliffs. Now that sounds very exciting, doesn't it?

Motorcycle racing
All over the world, there are people who enjoy motorcycle riding. Some people travel across continents on motorcycles because they find it fun and it relieves stress. But others are not interested in relaxing – they want an adrenalin rush, so they race motorcycles at very high speeds. They ride around a track at up to 300 kilometers per hour. When they go around a corner, they lean over so that their knees almost touch the ground, and they do that at about 200 kilometers per hour. That's fast!

So do you exercise to relax or do you take part in things to get that adrenalin rush?

16 Read **15** again and circle **T** for true and **F** for false.

1. Some extreme sports can give people an adrenalin rush. T F
2. Freeriders ski down very high, steep mountains. T F
3. Freeriders follow a path. T F
4. Freeriders and motorcycle racers want an adrenalin rush. T F
5. Freeriders and motorcycle racers aren't adventurous. T F

17 Find and circle the words in **14**.

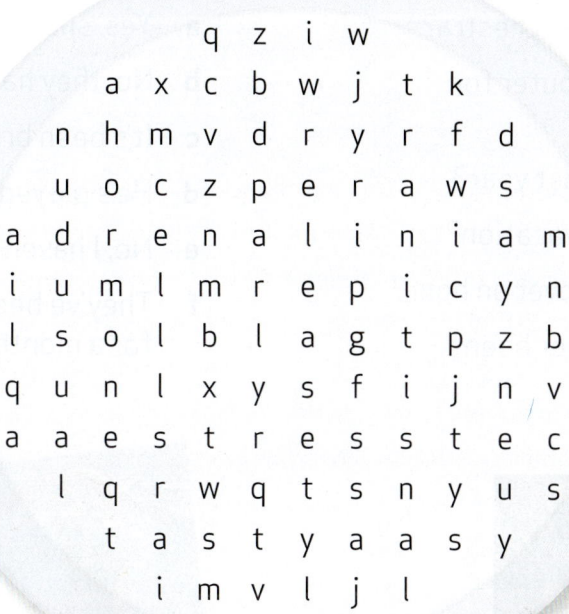

```
        q z i w
      a x c b w j t k
    n h m v d r y r f d
    u o c z p e r a w s
  a d r e n a l i n i a m
  i u m l m r e p i c y n
  l s o l b l a g t p z b
  q u n l x y s f i j n v
  a a e s t r e s s t e c
    l q r w q t s n y u s
      t a s t y a a s y
        i m v l j l
```

THINK BIG

What do you think? Check (✓) the extreme sports that give people an adrenalin rush.

Kitesurfing ☐   Hiking ☐

Deep sea diving ☐   Tennis ☐

Skydiving ☐   Skijoring ☐

Unit 9 **127**

Grammar

18 Read and circle.

1 He's lived in that house **for / since** 2011.
2 I've known her **for / since** five years.
3 We haven't seen our cat **for / since** four days.
4 Daphne has studied Italian **for / since** two months.
5 Have they read **for / since** half an hour?
6 Hasn't she been here **for / since** yesterday?

19 Read and match.

1 How long has he played in an orchestra?
2 Have you worked on the computer for two hours?
3 Has Teri lived in Paris since last year?
4 How long have they been on vacation?
5 Have they played soccer for over an hour?
6 How long has the roller coaster been broken?

a Yes, she has.
b No, they haven't.
c It's been broken since April.
d He's played for a year.
e No, I haven't.
f They've been on vacation for a month.

20 Complete the sentences. Use **for** or **since**.

1 We haven't visited our cousins _____ March.
2 Have you studied French _____ a long time?
3 Has she been in the bath _____ six o'clock?
4 You haven't read a book _____ Monday.
5 Have we waited here _____ that long?
6 Sam hasn't been camping _____ a year.

21 Put the words in the correct order.

1 ten years / him / we've / known / for
   _____

2 since / she / us / hasn't / last year / visited
   _____

3 a dancer / how long / you / been / have / ?
   _____

4 listened / to music / all day / he / has / ?
   _____

5 written / school / since / Yolanda / for the / has / grade / newspaper / ten
   _____

22 Answer the questions for you.

1 How long have you studied English?
   _____

2 Have you lived in your home for a long time?
   _____

3 How long have you known your best friend?
   _____

4 Has your family lived in your country since you were born?
   _____

Unit 9 **129**

Culture Connection | Around the World

23 Read and match.

1 parachute
2 professional
3 risk
4 extreme sports
5 warrior
6 trick

a brave soldier from a long time ago
b chance that something bad might happen
c something you do to entertain people
d piece of safety equipment worn by people jumping out of a plane
e sports that involve a high level of risk
f with a high level of skill, education, or training

24 Read and complete with the words from the box. Then listen and check.

achieved   extreme sports   goals   professional   risks   sail

Record-breaking Teenagers

1 All around the world, there are teenagers who do amazing things at home, at school, or on the sports field. But some teenagers take enormous ¹_____ and break records in the world of ²_____. Let's read about two record-breaking teenagers, who set out to achieve and succeed in reaching their amazing ³_____.

2 Jordan Romero is a ⁴_____ climber who, as a teenager, climbed seven of the highest and most challenging mountains on seven continents. He climbed his first mountain, Mount Kilimanjaro in Africa, in 2006 when he was ten years old. He's the youngest person in the world to do this. In 2011, when he was fifteen years old, he climbed the last of the seven mountains, a mountain in Antarctica. Jordan, who lives in California, wants to help other teenagers reach their goals, so he started a group called *Find Your Everest*.

3 In 2012, a Dutch teenager, Laura Dekker, became the youngest person to ⁵_____ around the world on her own. Laura has been on or near water all her life. She was born on a boat, got her first boat when she was six years old, and at eight years old began dreaming about sailing around the world. At ten years old, she got her second boat, *Guppy*, and at fifteen years old she set off on her long trip. A year and a day later, she ⁶_____ her goal. She was just sixteen years old. When Laura finished the trip and got off her boat, her mother, father, sister, grandparents, and many cheering fans greeted her.

25 Read 24 again and answer the questions.

1   How many mountains on how many continents has Jordan Romero climbed?
_____

2   How old was Jordan when he climbed his last mountain?
_____

3   What does *Find Your Everest* do?
_____

4   How old was Laura when she got her first boat?
_____

5   How old was Laura when she set off to achieve her goal?
_____

6   At sixteen years old, what record did Laura set?
_____

26 Complete the sentences with words from 23.

1   If you jump from a very high cliff into the ocean, you are taking a great _____.

2   Skydivers freefall for a while before opening their _____ to land safely.

3   Shaka Zulu was a famous African _____ who fought fierce battles against the English.

4   My uncle is a _____ sailor – he's a captain in the Royal Navy.

5   The aerialist performed an amazing _____ while balancing on a tightrope.

6   _____ have been around for centuries, as a way to prove strength.

THINK BIG

Pretend that you could interview one of the teenagers in 24. Which one would you interview? What two questions would you ask?

Who? _____

Question 1: _____

Question 2: _____

Unit 9 **131**

Writing | Description: Experience

A good description includes:
- a clear topic sentence that tells the reader what you are going to write about. Example: *I'm not a risk taker.*
- more information about the topic that gives examples or details. You can introduce your examples using *For example*. Always use a comma. *For example, I don't like trying new foods. I also get nervous when I go to new places where I can't speak the language.*
- a summary that retells your topic sentence in a new way. Example: *It's OK that I'm not a risk taker because it's good to have different people in the world.*

27 Read the description. Then answer the questions. Write the numbers.

> ¹I'm not at all adventurous, and I don't like to try new things. ²For example, I don't play sports because every time I've played, I've gotten hurt. ³I also don't like trying new foods, and I prefer to eat the same food every day. ⁴This is strange because my whole family loves trying food from different cultures. ⁵Everyone says I should be more adventurous and try new things, but I'm happy just the way I am.

_____ 1 Which sentence is the topic sentence?
_____ 2 Which sentences give details about the topic?
_____ 3 Which sentence retells the topic in a new way?

28 Think of ways that you are *not* adventurous. Complete the chart.

Complete the sentence: I am not adventurous because…
Give an example and details.
Give another example and details.
Write a summary. Explain in one sentence how you are not adventurous.

29 Write a paragraph about how you are *not* adventurous. Use 28 to help you.

Review

30 Find and circle these words.

```
            q z i w
        a x c b w j t k
    n o m v d q y r f d
    u d p z p a r a w s
    a n s o u r g h d i a m
    i u m p m r s p i c y n
    l s f u b l w g t p z b
    q u p l x y e f i j n v
    a a e a g l e d o t e c
    l q r w q t s n y u s
        t a s t y a a s y
            i m v l j l
```

| popular |
| raw |
| sour |
| spicy |
| sweet |
| tasty |
| traditional |
| unusual |

31 Complete the sentences. Use some of the words in **30**.

1 One soup at the Spanish restaurant has a lot of spices in it. Not many people order it.

   The soup is too _____, so it isn't _____.

2 Many of the dishes at the Greek restaurant are delicious seafood dishes. One of the dishes was eaten long ago, too.

   That seafood dish is _____ and _____.

3 The new Mexican restaurant has a dessert that is made with avocado and lime.

   The avocado pudding isn't common. It's _____. It isn't sweet like usual desserts. It's _____.

32 Complete the sentences. Use the correct form of the verb in parentheses. Then answer the questions for you.

1 _____ you ever _____ to a Japanese restaurant? (be)

   _____

2 _____ you ever _____ an octopus? (see)

   _____

3 _____ you ever _____ curry? (eat)

   _____

Unit 9 133

Checkpoint | Units 7–9

1 Unscramble and write the words. Add your own words on the extra lines.

GADGETS
1 _____
2 _____
3 _____
4 _____
5 _____

1 nattisn aecamr
2 hldenadh agem edievc
3 tniasrsort rdaoi
4 ivdoe aemg syetsm

PRODUCTS AND MATERIALS
1 _____
2 _____
3 _____
4 _____

1 tootnc janes
2 urrbeb botos
3 yacl

1 edusoiilc
2 lpruapo
3 tadiilnroat
4 uusulan

FOOD
1 _____
2 _____
3 _____
4 _____
5 _____

2 Find a song that talks about gadgets, products, and materials or food. Complete the chart about the song.

Song title	
Who's the singer?	
Where does the singer come from?	
Who was the song written by?	
What's your favorite line in the song? Why is it your favorite?	
Would the singer rather sing traditional songs or popular songs?	
Has the song ever been a number one hit?	
Who else do you think might sing the song well?	

3 Write a note to your parents. Persuade them to let you go to a concert to hear this song and singer. Use the information in 1 and 2 to help you.

Checkpoint Units 7–9 **135**

Unit 1 | Extra Grammar Practice

1 Read about Lisa and Dan. Complete the sentences with the correct words. Use the correct form of the verbs.

Lisa

"I'm in the drama club. I play the trumpet in the school orchestra. I can draw, but I can't paint. Soccer is fun, but basketball is boring."

"I'm in the math club. I want to learn how to do karate. Soccer is fun, but basketball isn't fun. I can't draw."

Dan

1 Lisa is good at _____. (draw/paint)
2 Dan is interested in _____. (act/learn karate)
3 They aren't interested in _____. (draw/play basketball)
4 They enjoy _____. (play soccer/play basketball)

2 Look at **1**. Complete the sentences with the words in parentheses.

1 Lisa _____. (good at/paint)
2 Dan _____. (enjoy/draw)
3 Dan _____. (like/do math)
4 Lisa _____. (love/play the trumpet)

3 Look at **1**. Complete the sentences with the correct form of the verbs in parentheses.

1 **Lisa:** How about joining the art club?
   Dan: No, thanks. I _____. (like)

2 **Dan:** Do you want to join the math club?
   Lisa: I don't think so. I _____. (interested in)

3 **Emily:** How about joining the soccer club?
   Dan and Lisa: Why not? We _____. (love)

4 **Brian:** Why don't you try out for the basketball team?
   Dan and Lisa: Definitely not! We _____. (enjoy)

Extra Grammar Practice | Unit 2

1 Complete the sentences. Use the correct form of the verbs in parentheses.

1  My parents _____ (get married) when they _____ (be) very young. A few months later, they _____ (move) to London.

2  My father _____ (open) his own restaurant in Brighton when I _____ (be) a teenager. I _____ (work) with my father every weekend. A few years ago, I _____ (help) my father open his second restaurant.

2 Read and draw the pictures. Then write the answers.

1 Alice is shorter than Carl. Barbara is taller than Alice but shorter than Carl.

Who's the tallest?

_____

2 Jose is younger than Frank. Frank is older than Edward. Edward is older than Jose.

Who's the youngest?

_____

3 My brother, Ted, is very strong. He's stronger than my dad. My dad is stronger than my mom. I'm Mark. I'm stronger than Ted.

Who's the strongest in the family?

_____

Unit 3 | Extra Grammar Practice

1 How could students help their school? Make suggestions. Use **could** and the words from the box.

> clean up the playground   paint the art room   plant trees

1. Sophia _____
2. Brian _____
3. Jilly _____

2 Unscramble the words. Then write sentences with **am/is/are going to**. What are these students going to do this week?

1. shaw arsc _____   We _____.

2. rweti alteircs _____   Peter and Jake _____.

3. abek sceak _____   I _____.

4. eakm sptrseo _____   Rebecca _____.

Extra Grammar Practice | Unit 4

1 Look at the chart. Complete the sentences. Use more/less ... than or the least/the most and the words in parentheses.

	Jeff	Tony	Silvia
Making a volcano	👍👍	👍👍	👍
Mixing liquids	👍	👍	👍👍
Making electricity	👍👍👍	👍👍	👍👍👍

How did the students feel about their science class experiments?

1 **Silvia:** Mixing liquids was _____ making a volcano. (interesting)

2 **Jeff:** Making electricity was _____ of all. (exciting)

3 **Tony:** Mixing liquids was _____ experiment. (amazing)

4 **Jeff:** Making a volcano was _____ making electricity. (challenging)

2 Look at 1. Write sentences. Use as ... as or not as ... as.

1 **Jeff:** Making a volcano / fun / making electricity.

_____

2 **Tony:** Making electricity / exciting / making a volcano.

_____

3 **Silvia:** Mixing liquids / interesting / making electricity.

_____

3 Look at 1. Write sentences. Use too or not enough and the words in parentheses.

1 **Silvia:** I didn't like making a volcano. It was _____. (interesting)

2 **Jeff:** Mixing liquids wasn't fun. It was _____. (boring)

3 **Tony:** I'm not interested in mixing liquids. It was _____. (exciting)

Unit 4 **139**

Unit 5 | Extra Grammar Practice

1 Match the puzzle pieces. Then complete the story. Use the sentences on the puzzle pieces and the correct form of the verbs.

Charlie's Silly Dream

- She / turn the pancakes
- Charlie / fall asleep
- his math book / sing him songs
- his backpack / began to fly
- Charlie / walk to school
- Charlie / have a snack
- The bananas / jog on the table
- the pancakes / start dancing

In the morning

Charlie's mother was making pancakes for breakfast.

1 _____ when _____.

"Time for school, Charlie," said his mom.

2 _____ when _____.

In the afternoon

Charlie was hungry.

3 _____ while _____.

At night

Charlie was doing his math homework. Then he got very tired.

4 _____ while _____.

His soccer ball turned off the light. "Goodnight, Charlie."

2 Circle the correct answers.

1 What was Charlie doing when his backpack began to fly?
   a He was walking to school.   **b** He walked to school.

2 What was his mom doing when the pancakes started dancing?
   a She was making breakfast.   **b** She made breakfast.

3 Was Charlie jogging when he had a snack?
   a No, he didn't.   **b** No, he wasn't.

4 Was he sleeping when the soccer ball turned out the light?
   a Yes, he was.   **b** Yes, he did.

Extra Grammar Practice | Unit 6

1 Read. Then complete the sentences. Use *no one* and *everyone*.

 One hundred years from now…

100 years from now, the world will be very different. ¹_____ will use smartphones because our phones will be inside our heads! ²_____ will use flying cars, and ³_____ will live in apartments in tall buildings in space. Not like today. Today, many people live in houses. In the future, ⁴_____ will live in houses any more. Machines will make our food at home and in restaurants. ⁵_____ will need to cook any more. ⁶_____ will study in schools because there won't be any school buildings, and we won't have teachers. ⁷_____ will study at home using computers.

2 Look at 1. Complete the sentences. Use *will* or *won't* and the verbs in parentheses.

1 There _____ any teachers. (be)
2 We _____ people with cell phones. (call)
3 We _____ in apartments in space. (live)
4 People _____ flying cars. (drive)
5 We _____. (cook) Machines _____ (cook) for us.

3 Match the sentences. Write the letters.

In the future…

___ 1 Students won't need teachers.
___ 2 We'll go to the moon on vacation.
___ 3 No one will go to friends' houses.
___ 4 Everyone will be happy.

a We'll meet by video messaging.
b They'll teach themselves.
c Nobody will be sad.
d Spaceship travel will be cheap.

4 Look at 3. Do you think these things will happen? Write your answers.

_____
_____
_____

Unit 7 | Extra Grammar Practice

1 Complete the sentences. Use *is*/*are used to* and the words from the box.

> eat   get around   protect eyes   write

1 A pencil _____.
2 Plates _____.
3 A bike _____.
4 Sunglasses _____.

2 What do you think these things are? Write sentences. Use *It may be* or *It might be*.

1
_____

2
_____

3
_____

4
_____

3 Answer the questions. Use the words in parentheses.

1 I'm thinking of something. It's round, and it bounces. People play a game with it. What do you think it is?
_____ (may)

2 I'm thinking of a type of sweet food. They're small and taste nice. They're often seen at birthday parties. What do you think they are?
_____ (might)

3 I'm thinking of a small insect. It likes hot, wet weather. It can fly, and it makes a noise when it flies. What do you think it is?
_____ (might)

Extra Grammar Practice | Unit 8

1 Complete the sentences. Use the correct passive form of the verb in parentheses.

1. The very first cookie _____ in about the 7th century in Persia. (invent)
2. Crops, such as rice and wheat, _____ in many countries today. (grow)
3. In 2005, a bowl of noodles four thousand years old _____ by scientists in China. (discover)
4. Bananas _____ in the Caribbean every year. (pick)
5. A lot of coffee _____ in Colombia these days. (produce)

2 Complete the puzzle. Write the letters. Use the words from the box.

> Africa   Argentina   Brazil   China
> invent   mine   produce   raise

1	2	3	4
_A_	_A_	_C_	_i_
_ m	_	_	_
_ _	_r_	_	_B_ _p_
d i a m o n d s	**c a t t l e**	**n o o d l e s**	**r u b b e r**
_ _	_ _	_	_ _
_	_ _	_	_ _
	_ _		_
			_

3 Look at 2. Write sentences. Use is/are or was/were and the words in the puzzle.

1. _____
2. _____
3. _____
4. _____

Unit 9 | Extra Grammar Practice

1 Look at the chart. Complete and answer the questions.

	fly to the U.K.	win a spelling quiz	ride a horse	visit China	eat octopus
Georgina	✓			✓	✓
Rob		✓	✓		✓

1 _____ Georgina ever _____ to the U.K.?
_____

2 _____ Georgina ever _____ a spelling quiz?
_____

3 _____ Georgina ever _____ China?
_____

4 _____ Rob ever _____ octopus?
_____

5 _____ Rob ever _____ a horse?
_____

Georgina

Rob

2 Read. Then complete and answer the questions.

> Tom and Sara like spicy food, adventurous sports, beaches, and adrenalin rushes. Karen likes unusual food, but she doesn't like hot spices, scary sports, mountains, or adrenalin rushes.

1 _____ Karen _____ eat spicy food or an avocado dessert?
_____

2 _____ Tom and Sara _____ visit a museum or ski down a mountain?
_____

3 _____ Sara _____ go swimming or mountain climbing?
_____

4 _____ Tom and Sara _____ ride a motorcycle fast or slowly?
_____

5 _____ Karen _____ ski fast down a mountain or walk in the woods?
_____

Young Learners English Practice
Flyers

Note to students:
These practice materials will help you prepare
for the YLE (Young Learners English) Tests.
There are three kinds of practice materials in this sampler:
Listening, Reading & Writing, and Speaking.
Good luck!

Young Learners English Practice Flyers: Listening A

– 5 questions –

 Listen and draw lines. There is one example.

Peter   Michael   Robert   Emma

Richard   David   Katy

Young Learners English Practice Flyers: Listening B

– 5 questions –

 Listen and write. There is one example.

Greenfields Camp

Where: _____ in the Peak District

1 **Activities:** _____

2 **How long:** _____

3 **Cost:** _____

4 **When the next camp begins:** _____

5 **What to bring:** _____

Young Learners English Practice Flyers: Listening C

– 5 questions –

 What do the Martins and the Browns like to do?

Listen and write a letter in each box. There is one example.

 Mrs. Martin

 Mr. Brown

 Kelly Martin

 David Martin

 John Brown

 Cindy Brown

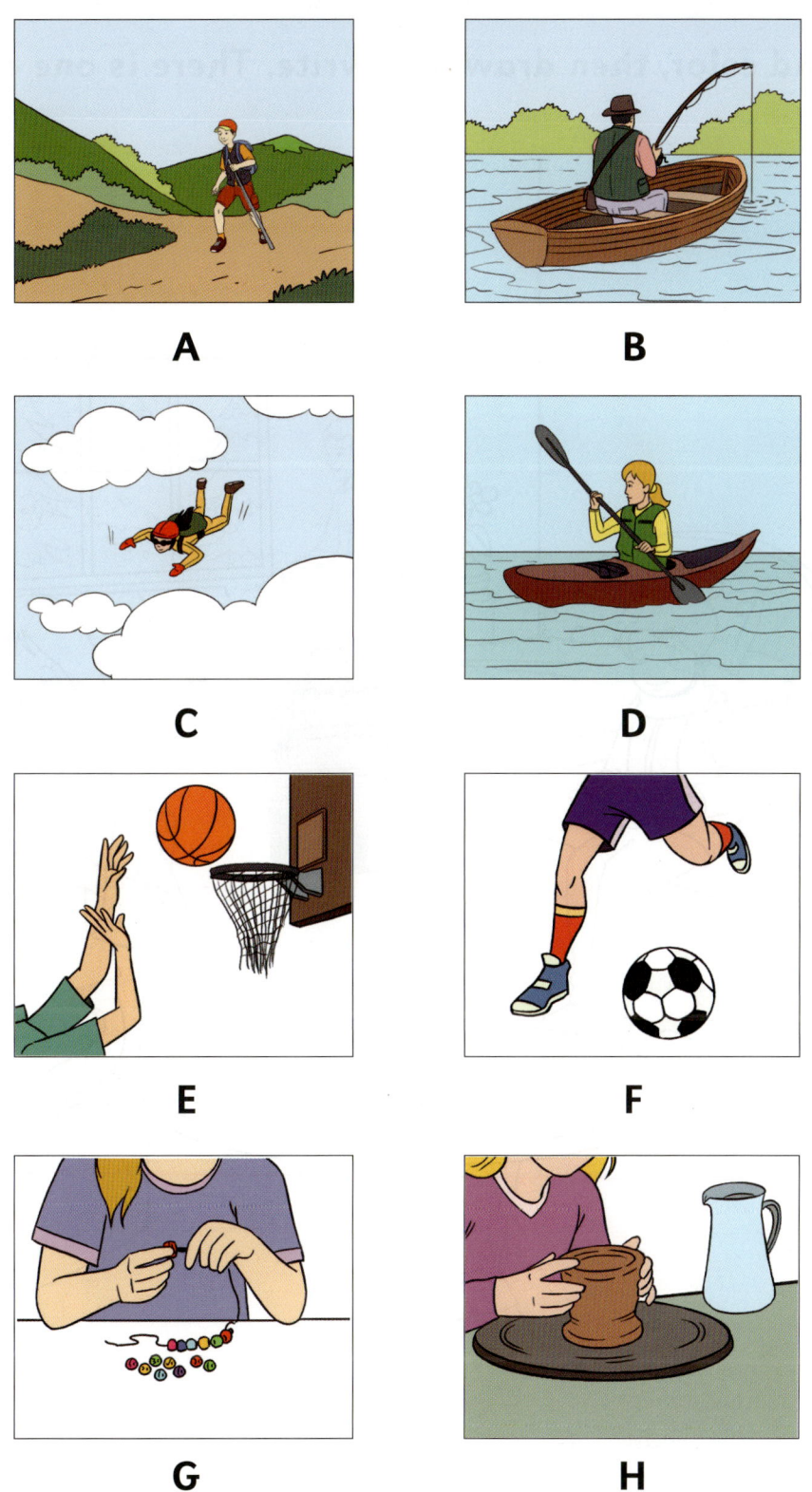

Listening C 149

Young Learners English Practice Flyers: Listening D

– 5 questions –

166

Listen and color, then draw and write. There is one example.

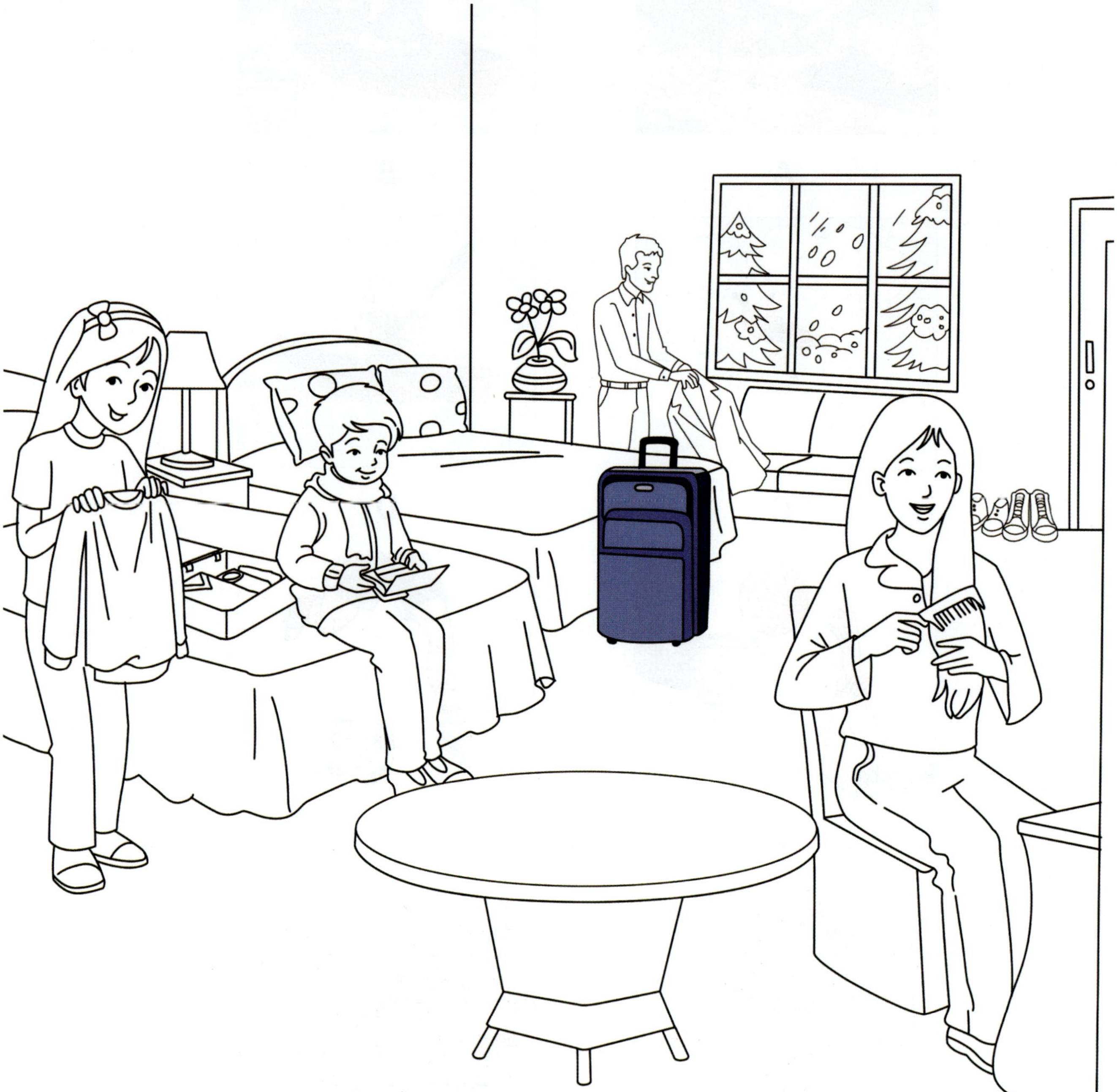

Young Learners English Practice Flyers: Reading & Writing A

– 10 questions –

Look and read. Choose the correct words and write them on the lines. There is one example.

aunt   delicious   bracelet   graduate

school orchestra

silver

expensive

insect repellent

drama club

a kayak

an article   cake sale   a smartphone

She's your father's sister. _____aunt_____

1 This group puts on plays. If you're an actor, you should try it! _____

2 If you're a musician and know how to play an instrument, this is the group for you. _____

3 You'll do this when you finish college. _____

4 You could write this to tell people about something your school club is doing to raise money. _____

5 Earrings or necklaces are often made of this. _____

6 When something tastes really nice, this is how it tastes. _____

7 Take this with you when you go hiking so mosquitoes won't bite you. _____

8 You can use this to listen to music, play games, or call someone. _____

9 You can ride in this kind of boat. It only fits one or two people. _____

10 We use this word to talk about something that costs a lot of money. _____

Young Learners English Practice Flyers: Reading & Writing B

– 6 questions –

Read the story. Choose a word from the box. Write the correct word next to numbers 1–5. There is one example.

Mark and his classmates entered a contest at a science fair. The contest was to see which team could create the most useful ___invention___. Mark's team created a (1) _____ that could clean an entire house. It could clean the living room (2) _____, too. The judges were impressed, but the other team also had a good idea. They showed off an (3) _____ that could store over 5,000 songs. Probably the most interesting thing about it was its source of power. It didn't use a (4) _____. It was (5) _____. The problem was you had to leave it in the sun every day for three hours. The judges didn't think that was practical, so Mark and his team won.

Example

| invention | battery | speakers | spaceship | solar-powered |
| MP3 player | robot | laptop | radio | furniture |

(6) Now choose the best name for the story.

Check (✓) one box.

Inventions Through History ☐

Two Heads Are Better Than One ☐

A Winning Idea ☐

Young Learners English Practice Flyers: Reading & Writing C

– 8 questions –

Read the text. Choose the correct words and write them on the lines.

Costa Rica – Land of Adventure!

Example	Costa Rica is a country in Central America. Costa Rica is ___Known___ for its many beautiful beaches, mountains, and forests. It is
1	_____ by millions of people every year.
2	People go to Costa Rica _____ see amazing animals and to be close to nature. But there are
3	many _____ activities in Costa Rica, too.
4	Have you _____ heard of ziplining?
5	A zipline is a long wire. It's _____ of metal.
6	A zipline is used _____ traveling from one place to another, high above the ground. You can
7	ride on a zipline in the forest _____ go
8	from tree to tree. Are you _____? Maybe ziplining is for you!

154 Reading & Writing C

Example	know	knew	known
1	visit	visiting	visited
2	in	for	to
3	unusual	spicy	delicious
4	done	ever	had
5	did	made	invent
6	to	then	for
7	doing	for	to
8	terrible	different	adventurous

Young Learners English Practice Flyers: Speaking A

Find the differences **Candidate's copy**

Young Learners English Practice Flyers: Speaking A